Clarity

Author

Suzanne Massee

© Suzanne Massee 2018.

ISBN – 978-0-6483420-4-5 Paperback

ISBN – 978-0-6483420-0-7 eBook

Suzanne Massee is

the author of

Amplify Thoughts

Thoughts Create

Conversations with Consciousness

Back to Basics

Back to Basics Harvest

Suzanne's Easy to Follow Baking Recipe's

Table of Contents

Acknowledgement 7
Suzanne's synopsis 9
Clarity 10
Imagination is the only success 11
Introduction 12
Author 19
Infinite Intelligence Orchestrating My Events 29
Joy 41
Evidence of Joy 45
In Physical Vibration 45
Miracles 73
Disruption of Religion 77
Laws of the Universe 91
Law of Attracting Alignment 91
Law of Thought 101
Law of Want 105
Law of Feelings and Emotions 113
Law of Alignment of Allowing 119
The All Knowing 125
Love 133
Being in Oneness 133
Inspiration 137
Inspired Action 137

Health and Well-Being 141
I Want a Different Body 149
Education -Work – Business 153
Finding a Vibrational Partner 163
Dreams 169
Consciousness and Infinite Intelligence 169
Harmonizing Words 173
Daily Intentions 180
Scripting Selection Intentions 182
Scripting Creative Imagination 183
Thrive 185
Thrive Momentum Phrases 189
Moods 197
Being more 201
Focus 203
Define Feelings 206
Appreciation 208
Conditions I am facing 211
Solution to a problem 213
Being non- resistant 215
Abundance 219
Whatever is happening today 223
Allowing 226
I am ready 231

Create Un-Limitedness 236
Think, Feel and Focus 238
Being a Conscious Deliberate Creator or Being the Default Creator 242
You are being watched 247
Suzanne's Thriving Phrases 250
Imagination 254
Riding the Wave 259
More Inspiring Books by the Author 265
Social media 271
My positive momentum phrases 272

Acknowledgement

I appreciate all the manifest-able individuals who co-created in my experiences for my expansion. Even when experiences took me down many roads it was the beginning process of me, and for them all, to become more connected to whom they want to become with their own unique Inner Beings.

With the expansion I achieved through my experiences, I became abundantly appreciative with the whole of me, and being in alignment with me and my Inner Being, and with this discovery I would like to guide you to the core of who you are meant to be and feel the clarity through your own emotions.

There is nothing more profound than your Inner Being, your Soul, your Sprit, your Spiritual Self, The Self, The Source; this is the reason for the adage pronunciation of capitalising the relevant importance of expressing the words used.

My deepest appreciation that created and took my expansion to new heights was the teachings by Abraham, infinite intelligence in the non-physical working through Esther Hicks in the physical. Nothing is more pleasing than to listen to Abraham and to tune into an even higher vibrational energy.

It is the supreme art of the teacher to awaken joy in creative expression and knowledge.

: Albert Einstein

Suzanne's synopsis

It is a repetition of speaking, repetitive words in writing, and it is all in the repetitive thoughts, it is through repetition that some form of recognition will finally attune you into your Source your Inner Being, re-read and re-read the connection will, and does happen, it is all up to you and you alone.

Clarity

Clarity is lining up with something that is really clear and I like it, it makes me feel good.

Clarity is in the transformation of the contrast into better feeling thoughts, not to avoid the negative thoughts but to transform and emphasis new better thoughts which makes me feel good.

Imagination is the only success

You are bringing the reality in, of which is in your imagination of what you want, in other words reality does not exist, it is the thoughts that bring about the reality. Reality only exists if you keep on perpetuating it. Reality then becomes the wanted or unwanted desires.

Introduction

Read not to contradict and confute, nor to find talk and disclosure, but to weigh and consider

: Francis Bacon

We are all vibrating energy and receiving vibrational energy that is perceived in and by the non- physical part of you which resides within you, which you call your Soul, or Spirit, or Spiritual Self, or Your Inner Being, and it is felt in the here and now in the physical reality of The Self. You can never detach or disconnect from this vibration, it exists forever, even in death, and re-emerges again and again. It is the energy life stream of your many life time experiences and it is forever building to an even greater expansion of your Inner Being. You are all intertwined in this collective conscious energy stream, not separate from it.

I and We have chosen to come forth into this life time to experience expansion and growth for our Source energy our Inner Being, which resides within, and most of all to remember that we are all extensions of this Source energy forever changing and expanding.

This growth is the expansion of our own emotional vibrational energy stream, with each emotional process that we experience, creates an expansion of energy within our own Inner Being. This energy expands experientially out into the Universe and becomes a greater expansion of your Inner Being and to the Source which; is this stream of energy that flows to you and through you, and this energy expands experientially out into the Universe and becomes a greater expansion of your Inner Being.

We are here to create; you and I have come here to evolve as deliberate manifesting creators. The deliberate creator intentionally intends its intentions and manifesting into his/her experience via the intentions of the inner consciousness Your Inner Being, and the non-physical infinite collective intelligence energies of the universe. This energy exists, this collective intelligence energy is with you always, if your intentions is asking with powerful wanting of being a scientist, call upon a scientist energy of i.e. Albert Einstein, if you want to be a painter call upon one of the energies i.e.; Leonardo da Vinci or Picasso, they all exist and are eager to clarify and guide your path your thoughts. This energy exists and can be called upon even with a living physical being for interaction and clarification; it is the exchange of Collective Consciousness of vibrational energy. If you have a strong calling for value and enhancement for your Inner Being, it begins with the thought, and in the quiet moments you have in thought, are they your thoughts? Or the stream of Infinite Intelligence energy, giving thought to the ideas.

This stream is powerful; it is the discrediting of your thoughts and what you have been taught, by other individuals that have no idea of this energy stream.

It is not to understand the stream, but to know it exists. To understand or make sense of it, takes you further away from it.

When you come to the decision and acknowledge that this life stream exists, and it exists in how you feel, it then begins the opening of the portals to more information, to more solutions, to more clear thinking to the outcomes, to the desires, and to feeling more into greater detail of your internal emotions, is where it all resides. You don't turn on the light switch and ask how did you get here, how does this power make light, you just trust the power is making light, this is the same power that is vibrating through every living person, nature and animals, the difference between man and animal is the animals work with this vibrating energy always, they intuitively know, whereas man has lost touch with this intuitive energy. The intuitive part of you just knows, how you know is all up to you, and that is getting to know you, with You.

We all begin our lives to be the deliberate manifesting creator, we all came forth and were eager to play the game and have fun along the way, and then life takes over and what you came forth to do in this life time is forgotten, at some point in time you begin to question what is life, for some life takes a turn that becomes so significant that you begin to question what you came here for, and for those it is the starting point of tuning your vibration back to what you first intended to do when you made the transition from the non-physical into the physical, and that is to be in fine attunement with your life stream your Inner Being, and to remember that you are The Source you are eternal, you are the creator, and can, and are all able to manifest your wants and desires, and above all, to have joy and fun in this life time experience.

This is a vibrational universe, we are here to remember our own emotional guidance system, and we are here to tap into the indicators of this emotional guidance. Once you get it, it is so easy; it takes discernment of your relationship of your emotions, feelings and thoughts, and to what vibrational atmosphere you are activating to these emotions.

Through a process of fine tuning your emotional vibrational frequency with your Inner Being you will attain clarity, clarity will become your vibrational discernment of emotions into how you are feeling, and to where you are pointing your attraction of the momentum of thought, to the wants and don't wants.

Clarity becomes the indicator of the contrast that you are feeling with those thoughts; every thought has a contrasting thought; it is deciphering the contrasting thought and to what thought continuation you want to hold and maintain.

The Source your Inner Being greatly enhances well-being and expansion of thoughts and desires through the process of pure thought, appreciative thoughts, appreciation into the feelings of the thought, and the appreciation of the appreciation, through the intentions of that thought, through the intentions of the feelings and the emotions, through unconditional appreciation, through unconditional love, through joy, through the words that create harmony and create up lift meant, through creating an atmosphere of the story, your desired story into a vibrational imagination of thought, and bringing this story into fruition, through appreciation regardless of the conditions of the present now. It is <u>You</u> being in the fullness with <u>You</u> in the present Now, in all that you do whether it be viewing, eating, speaking, relaxing, thinking, or observing, this is you rendezvousing with your Inner Being.

This is a time of creating a clean-up of your vibration, which creates the path of no resistance to the desired wants that you have been building momentum too.

We all came forth eagerly and deliberately to expand and achieve momentum of thought, and to decipher contrast and alignment, most of all to align and remember the older wiser part of you which has lived and experienced many eternal reality life paths, reaching for the fulfilment of pure wholeness and becoming more, and expanding more.

I was asked why I use the word 'Source'

From a very young age I knew deep inside of me that I was and am, what is called God, but the God word never felt right to me, it implies religion, it made me feel very uncomfortable, I used to call it the <u>G</u>reat <u>of</u> <u>d</u>ivine a changed version of God, it wasn't until I heard the word Source and Source energy I immediately tuned into me, no question it was instant. I prefer to use the term Source, or Inner Being. Source separates you from the prevalent teachings of what God is, there is only one God and that is you in all its pureness, to say that you are God is blaspheme in the eyes of religious teachings, and becomes the separateness of who you really are. This is the momentum process of the religious system which has created disunity, confusion and separateness within these teachings of who and what God is.

'I consecrate myself to meet their <u>need for growth in truth and Holiness</u>, I am not praying for these alone but also for the <u>future believers'</u> John 17: 19-21TLB

'Is it not written in the scriptures <u>ye are all Gods'</u> Psalm 82.6

'Love the lord <u>your</u> God with all <u>your</u> heart and all <u>your</u> soul and with all <u>your</u> mind and with all <u>your</u> strength' Mark 12:30.

The word <u>your</u> is taken out of context and distorted of the use of the word <u>your</u> which is a word used to indicate that <u>one belonging to oneself</u>. The kingdom of heaven is within; or (in your midst) Just taking a simple word and exaggerating it into a great almighty apart from you has taken <u>you</u> apart from <u>you</u>, You have separated yourself from who you really are, and that is you are God, not separate from it, but an extension of this stream of energy.

When creating you feel inferior in your creating, because after all that what you call God creates worlds, it is Y<u>ou</u> who Y<u>ou</u> are, as what man calls God here by virtue expanding and creating this world with your vibration and your thoughts, you have come here to be meaningful to this world and to fulfil the reason of being, and being the whole of who you are to the greater expansion of you and with your Inner Being, you are an extension of this collective conscious energy vibrational stream, you flow it, you are intertwined in this energy stream, and you are The Source (God), you are this life stream, and only you can dictate with you.

To really know God is to know how you feel, it is to know how you speak, it is to know how you think, it is know how you live, it is to know how to have fun, it is to know how to live joyfully, it is to know how to live happily, it is to know how you act, when you understand this simple logical interaction of communication between you and you, this is speaking to God, and when this understanding happens, and you begin being the receiver and feeling this energy, and then watch the results, you will create an expansion so powerful within.

'The kingdom of heaven is within' Luke 17-21

Author

The first step in the acquisition of wisdom is silence, the second listening, the third memory, the fourth practice, the fifth teaching others

: Solomon Ibn Gabriol

I was just a normal person, living a normal existence - or so I thought - until I had a near death experience - the experience of a marriage breakup, which capitulated into a vast amount of legal work, involving the family court and taking a lawyer to court, to self-learning and producing my own court documents, and on top of all of this, the disintegration of the family unit.

I had a strong asking, and this put me onto the solid road of the opening up to the inner consciousness, I experienced firsthand visions, voices, and outside forces of relayed messages, and this deep all-knowing.

I could have joined the different energy vibration of my very own family, but it was not a momentum that I wanted in my vibration. At the time life sucked and I was very hurt, I took solace in that it was a journey we all came here to experience, and how we achieve or accomplish a greater experience of The Self in this experience. I came to a greater realisation through the understanding of vibration, and that through the assistance of the family and all the relationships we have, were all in agreement and in the plan which we had created before we came forth into this phase of our life time living in the reality, it was for all our expansions, and with which momentum of thought patterns we decided to choose, by deliberately creating or creating by default.

I came to an experience of 'Clarity' of letting go of thoughts that were not serving me or the universe. Once the 'Clarity' came into focus that we are infinite and that the co-operative components of infinite intelligence surround us. I then achieved the wave of new desires the wave of advanced dreams. The understanding that the story was already completed, it is holding in vibration for me to come into alignment with the desires to bring about the activation, and manifest into full fruition. This is my story, telling what is now and what is coming to me. This emotional guidance vibration is so sophisticated, and yet so simple, it is the sophisticated mood guidance, the worse you feel the worse the feeling will replicate, and the better you feel the better the feeling will expand. As I became more I opened up more, the more I opened, the more I let in of the Source, until I held a steady vibration of feeling so good and so knowing that I allowed the universal forces to deliver in the perfect timing my desires. I am the realiser and the conscious deliberate creator of my feelings, and my desires. I allowed momentum to build within my whole beingness to the point I was riding the wave consistently. I am before you in this moment the achiever of such perfection of truly who I am; I know as each moment comes about there will be new clarifying moments and new desires.

I achieved all these manifested feelings and each manifestation became a clarifying manifestation until the momentum was so indescribable that it became the expectation of my desires, this is being truly the conscious deliberate creator.

The all-important secret to life is give up the opinions of everything, they are only opinions, their opinions, her opinions, his opinions, political opinions, or your opinions wrapped up in the opinions, they are only opinions to whomever the thoughts that have created it. Sift out the opinions, which does not serve you release them. The only opinion is to feel good and maintain this emotion and just keep reaching for the best feeling thought always- always- always.

Deep inside of me I always knew I was on this great path, I always knew I was going to inspire, teach and be an up-lifter to many people. I always had this deep residing knowing that the God that was being projected and portrayed was not what I thought of God, I always knew there was a greater aspect to what we were being told, how can there be an underlining God, when in the non-physical realm I receive clear visions of past life great mentors, and masters giving signs and indications. We all have access to these masters, these masters are prompting impulses, these impulses flow to you, it is whether you are in resistance to the impulses, or you are going with the flow of those impulses.

I always felt we can and are able to tap into this resourceful realm of the past life non-physical entities. I always felt it was not of a single energy of God, but of many, many collective energies, whether in the physical or the non-physical.

How can a voice a minute before my accident tell me there was going to be an accident? Where did this come from? I started to question I wanted answers, to this unseen non-physical universe, there is something greater here than any physical being can begin to understand, unless you are finely tuned in with the non-physical universe, and The Source within, which expands this powerful vibrational energy, which flows interwoven vibrational energies throughout everything and everyone. This vibrational energy feels it feels emotions; it feels your vibrational energy. This vibration is looking and feeling through the eyes of your Inner Being, these eyes only see purity, only see good in all, no matter what they are doing or whatever the conditions, these eyes appreciate implicitly, when you are connected to your Inner Being, life is good and the more good you feel the more good will come.

I knew from an early age to say it better or think it better, I used to mull over in my mind after the fact that I should have done it better or said it better, I always had the philosophical approach 'Beauty lies within' and 'Don't do to others that you would not do unto you' so I knew then about the laws of the universe, this was then taken over in the cog mire of living and parenting, but deep down trying to find me, and reasons of being who I am or meant to be until my near death experience.

I had to go through greater losses, to eventually shifting countries, even though through each event the doors just opened, I was flowing in the right direction, but I was still no closer to my realisation of my desires. I then came to the realisation of what I was wanting was not really what I was wanting. I was shown in my vision years ago speaking to large amounts of people, but I had gone down a negative path and did not want to speak on this very topic of the Source energy, how can one speak about it when I was no closer to any acknowledgement of my manifested future outcomes.

I dived into the negative thought patterns, then into positive thought patterns but my outcome was going further into the void of nothing, praying and asking for guidance for my outcome to improve, asking questions why - how - when. I know what was meant to happen, how can, this be so hard, nothing is working.

Here I am on this merry go round, until I woke up early one morning and just started placing appreciation big time in my thoughts, I felt my very core expand, and then within hours I was given a vision of a book and it just sent me to another realm, I knew I was writing, now I am so inspired. I prepared the templates and I am ready to write. I start to write the book of 'Clarity' when I suddenly got this huge pain in my chest, being finely tuned in I knew straight away that it was not time yet, I stopped writing and instantly the pain just disappeared. When it was time to write a couple of weeks later the fingers just flowed and my book 'Clarity' evolved. I feel so powerfully tuned in with my Source, I feel this book was all lined up to evolve the expansion of me and my fine attunement of me, and in this expansion my greatest desire is to be an up-lifter, and to create the atmosphere for others to discover the core of who they really are.

The only part of this expansion journey, could I have produced my manifestations earlier, if I was tuned into my true vibration of me, or is it all to do with timing, or the right timing, or fine tuning my desires and the expansion of what I created for me in my vibrational escrow.

I believe it is a process of what you want and when you know what you want, you can feel the enlightening powerful energy within coming into being. I began to feel an ease within me even when some experiences came into being did not eventuate, I came to recognise I was having experiences to expand my expansion with even greater clarity, and how I was feeling in with that experience that had come into play, and how I observed the signs, and my relationship with my Inner Being, my Source.

I discovered the clarity of the universal laws between the feelings and the emotions on all the subjects relating to the wants and don't wants. I learnt to go into the feelings on any given momentum of thought pattern. I understood that clarity was not the disappointer on an outcome but the insight to take me to a higher vibration. I learnt to listen to my thoughts, and to the thoughts that came through out of the blue, I learnt that these thoughts were building a momentum of thought into clarity. I learnt that the condition that was present in the now was evolving my vibration to an even greater clarity. I was the realiser to love the persons around my present conditions unconditionally, and to discern the split energies of individuals, and to love them as they are, and they are all doing really well and will find their own attunement. I came to realise to let go and allow that the resolution to a situation will prepare the energies to flow through to a solution. I came to realise that the mirroring of the conditions was preparing my vibration into the wholeness and further clarity of who I am. I came to the realisation of letting go of the resistance when I was observing the now condition and reset the tone of the condition. I let go and focused myself into my desires, and I imagined my desires, I was living in my desires and creating an atmosphere absent of resistance, resistance meaning that it was not here yet. I came to further clarity that I was celebrating in great proportions of joyfulness within and I felt good, I entered the vibration of feeling the emotions, and the better I felt, the better I felt, even though no manifestations were realised in the here and now, I was feeling good in the knowing that it is already here. This is what creation is, deliberately creating and loving being the deliberate creator, loving building the imagination of your new story and then expanding that creational story, feeling it into a total feeling emotional vibration, and not giving up, or making it too hard, and or placing negative slants to the creation. Once you are tuned in, you become a powerful observer, a powerful deliberate observer, and you feel this ease expanding within, and you have this blissful glow that is pulsating within, you have this feeling that the whole of you has come into this joyful alignment, you feel a deep abiding love for yourself, you feel the beauty within, and know the beauty you hold, you feel this fullness within, your thoughts and expressions are constantly tuning into the frequency with emphasis on emotional feeling words and holding onto and maintaining this vibration, most of all it is the growth of feeling your own your Inner Being, and to remember that you are The Source (God) and are the willing representative of your expansion, your growth, this is the achievement we are all wanting to achieve, and then your desires will be realised. It is just a wonderful feeling and isn't it glorious to realise that everything in life is an easement and fine tuning of your expansion and resonating with your Source in such fullness, and the clarity of this expansion is so - so deliciously satisfying.

Words cannot teach, it is your own guidance system within you that is the powerful interaction between you and you, once you get it then life will evolve into more desires, and more contrasting experiences and more clarity, and will forever keep on evolving.

I expanded further into the development of feelings within me of a peaceful flow of knowing all that I have placed in my desires was already in the is-ness. I felt the emotional peaceful pulsating energy within me, and I glowed with its rightness. It is a feeling of being pregnant and the pulsating glow that you feel within, and it is the same feeling when you are about to deliver, it is the period of everything coming together just before the delivery and the preparation you suddenly feel inspired to do in readiness, it is an indescribable feeling that words cannot express, it is a feeling that you get too, and once you get it; it truly is the most perfect emotional manifestation. It is in the gestation period where the building of your dreams is created and forming, it is feeling the story into being, and living and reviling in the desire, where it becomes such a practised thought and is normal to think about and be happy with every detail of your desires, this is when the delivery of the manifestation becomes a reality. For me I felt it was an expectation, it was the next logical step, I built my dream, I reviled in my dream, I changed and enhanced my dream, I grew with each enhancement, I wrote my path, I dreamed big, I felt and experienced emotions and what each emotion was indicating. Even though nothing had changed, what had changed was my happiness within me, I felt the fullness, and it became and felt normal.

This emotional guidance vibration is so sophisticated, and yet so simple, it is the sophisticated mood guidance, the worse you feel the worse the feeling will replicate, and the better you feel the better the feeling will expand, and when you are in a place of alignment where conditions are occurring, and you can stand in a place of not reacting to the conditions but observing from a place of no resistance, this is achieving the art of alignment.

As I became more I opened up more, the more I opened, the more I let in of the Source, until I held a steady vibration of feeling so good and so knowing that I allowed the universal forces to deliver in the perfect timing my desires.

Even though I have experienced, and experienced what I have experienced, I sincerely appreciate all that I have experienced will be the beginning momentum of your own understanding and clarity for you to evolve into a brighter being and a fuller you. The realisation is such a positive vibration, such a positive momentum.

If I told you I wrote every detail in this book of Clarity while living in conditions that were far from any description of a person that could conceive the potential of any outcome or believe in the validation of truth or even proof to come into being, you would not even consider to read or listen or believe in my story, and if it were not for the validation you still would not believe, well believe me, my story, my words, and my alignment to the laws of the universe, I created my imagination into reality, you can do as I have done through the clarity of my example. If this were all conceivable then you can do as I have done, it takes the power of your thoughts and consistently aligning the thoughts to the NOW, not rehashing the past, and only thinking the projection and anticipation of the imagination of what you want in the future and what you want for you, and focusing only on feeling the emotions to the thoughts.

Prepare your vibration and then you will be the realiser of your desires.

Infinite Intelligence Orchestrating My Events

The true sign of intelligence is not knowledge but imagination

: Albert Einstein

Infinite intelligence orchestrates events either within minutes or events to come, this is guidance coming forth to evolve the way to the path for you, don't discount them, but observe and work to that flow. What stops the events from becoming is only with the discounted or negative thoughts to the event.

I was wanting to learn more and how to meditate and make connection after my near death experience, I joined a group, and the lady involved with the group asked me, 'Why are you here' 'I want to learn' I said, for her to promptly say 'You are far more advanced than us' I thought she was totally on a different planet! She had felt what was in my vibration.

Within this same group I was given this message from a lady who does automatic writing; this is the message from her vibrational guide which was channelled to her to give this message to the recipient being me; This was in 2008 and it confirmed to me what I discovered that week what I wanted to do, which was to teach and speak;

Well my dear Suzanne you are a dark horse. You have come leaps and bounds of late and we challenge you further. You need to take care of No:1 first and you know who this is. You have come a long path to get you here and many wouldn't even know the half of it! You are going to become one of our spiritual speakers and I feel you know this already. Your time has come to move forth in your plans. Your wisdom is greatly needed, and it will shine through. Many who have travelled this path have failed but you are turning it all around and people will flock to hear what you have to say.

Take this path journey as it will not be in disharmony for all those who will listen will be greatly inspired by you. You are a well deserving person who needs to know that others will take your role and fight for what they believe in. Well done for taking this stand. It is good and we are all so proud of you. Take advantage where they play best out for you and the love of spirit will guide you to where you need to be and when. Venture forth my dear child; you have a lot to give. Well done!

This message was channelled by Sheryl in Nelson New Zealand.

I shifted to Tauranga in New Zealand and all the events just kept on opening doors, even when I arrived in Tauranga. I felt uncomfortable at my sisters place on the first night, I had my bird and was told he had to stay at the front door, and all I said was 'Gooey I am so sorry, we will get out as soon as possible', to receive a phone call the next day from the house sitting place I was going to stay at, that they made a mistake and wanted me the next day. Talk about manifestation! When the house sit came to an end I found a rental accommodation but had no money to bring my furniture up from Nelson, and then I received in the mail a cheque for the amount needed by the court restorative justice for my accident which I had been receiving small amounts only. Talk about manifestations! The day I shifted into my rental and was unpacking I received a call from a lady looking for accommodation another manifestation because I had to supplement my income with a roommate, and she became a wonderful teacher on learning the New Age of spirituality, she took me on the journey of reading signs, seeing, hearing and being the observer. For her she was told by her inner guides to go to New Zealand from England, as she said 'I am a teacher and kick starter to those special souls, I was meant to be here to help you on your journey'.

Together we opened up a spiritual centre to teach, I always felt this direction was not my path and everything unfolded to hand the centre over to another person, and another significant message came through on the last evening event. The medium on platform came to me with an outstanding message in 2009 which provided focus when I was orchestrating negative thoughts within

Huge changes and you can cope with it as you are not given anything you cannot handle. New job, whole new way, and out with the old. New opportunities, amazing choices for you, fabulous! And you will look at them like a travel book and pick where you want to go, it is awesome!

She was showing hands of such openness and such vocalised voice of excitement!

Get your job first the rest will just follow on. Choose your occupation. You will find what you want to do. Temporary for this and saw internet with spirituality going from airy fairy to a structured way, so you will live and breathe it. Changes all around. I have three people here I normally have one. I have grand mum and great aunt and male guide. Well done and enjoy what is coming for you.

This message was relayed to me by Jenni B from Hamilton New Zealand.

I happened to be in the company of an English psychic who brought through the energy of my grand dad, she said 'I have this powerful energy here and he is saying his name is Peter, he is saying you are going to speak, but you have to know how you are going to speak.' My grand dads name was Pieter.

All these orchestrated messages became very significant for me to keep focused, more so when I was filling the void with negative thoughts and living without joy. I had to make the transition from this energy of thought as it was not serving me at all, into studying the universal energy of Abraham flowing thoughts through Esther Hicks and putting the laws into motion and feeling every emotion. The internet became my university of the universal teachings. I have never been into airy fairy spiritualism very much into the study of the universal laws and then feeling the laws and living the laws. I have always known my path and when you know something or a thing you know should happen and it is not happening, this does bring in doubt and this is why so many people leave the flow of the path, I had to find the vibrational energy and I knew it was coming but never knew when, and I did take the various paths of in alignment and out of alignment, these were all instrumental in bringing me into the whole of who I am and readying me into my purpose. It is the process of the unfolding, it is the process of experiencing, it is how you live and feel in the process, it is the process of pre-paving and focusing on the dream, and being in synch with the thoughts, and it is being accustomed with and having the decisive thoughts to the dream. I am here to up-lift and teach, this is me, and that is why the universe orchestrates significant messages along the way I just had to acclimate and find the way to the vibration and maintain this vibration in focused purity. I knew the process was coming together when I arrived at my voluntary work and three books came into the warehouse, the very best teachings by Abraham Hicks; this is truly being in alignment. Manifestations come in many forms as simple as my grandchild, all of seven years old, asking me about gluteus maximus, why this was so wonderful is that, while I was swimming my lengths, I kept on getting gluteus maximus, and I was thinking was there something wrong or work the muscle more , but what it was, was the universal energies relaying a thought form word that I will hear again, and by a very unlikely source of my seven year old grandchild asking me about gluteus maximus, when you are connected to this life stream you then understand it was a message for either keep on going or we are acknowledging you, but for so many they disregard such incredible information coming to them, and they say it is just a coincidence, nothing is a coincidence, just wake up and begin to observe.

I woke up one morning and had this feeling pervading through me things were happening. Sometime later I received a persistent song by ELO The telephone, and I knew without a doubt I was ready. The telephone meaning more thoughts are coming in, I am in alignment to receive more, and I can feel it.

Albert Einstein was my first clear vision I had clairvoyantly or seen through the third eye of my Inner Being, recently I have been drawn too and seeing his face in pictures and articles, and then on the television it was all about the discovery of his theory. During the night I woke up and thoughts came through that I had to write down.

'You are bringing the reality in, of which is in your imagination of what you want, in other words reality does not exist, it is the thoughts that bring about the reality. Reality only exists if you keep on perpetuating it. Reality then becomes the wanted or unwanted desires.'

The true sign of intelligence is not knowledge but imagination: Albert Einstein

Imagination and finding the vibration to the imaginative thought is the only key to success.

I sifted and sorted what I wanted, I went through many changes until I honed into the feeling of feeling the perfection of my imaginative dream desires, and it felt so right and it felt like eagerness, it felt joyful, it felt like a lot of fun in the imagination, it felt fun building upon and building upon the dream, even though it was not here I felt it. I savoured all the details and the most significant of all; I was having fun building the dream, it is all about the journey and how you live and feel within the journey, and that my dear friends is being the deliberate creator and creating the desire into full manifestation.

This brings me to another powerful emotional manifestation. I kept on getting through thought a song 'Only love can hurt like this' and I was wondering what this was for! In my own emotional vibration I had some cleaning up to do with what I was observing physically for some time, this all came to a culmination and I felt the emotional build up, and the momentum was off and running, it was an awful feeling, and I was having difficulty moving it, until I made some create by default choices, to make a change of this situation or to bring about a solution, of which was the wrong way, but this placed me on another vibration, to disregard what was happening physically, but to place my vibrational emotions into another manifested emotion of separateness, and then leaving it up to the universe to play out which scenario is the best choice for me, and when I placed a little thought back to the observing I kept on getting Christmas merriment songs. All these emotional manifestations are stronger experiences for more alignment and letting go of the resistance that is being held onto, for cleaning up the vibration, and to observe differently, it is standing apart within, and to feel a disconnect-ness, but a disconnect-ness of believing your dream and pretending that it is already here. On a funny note this is what people would say; she needs psychological help, or it is a mental issue, or be realistic, or face the real world.

It is finding pleasure in the conditions and to feel good and the desires of wants that you have been dreaming of will come to you. You have to be happy with the prospect of your imaginative dreams, be happy with everything; everything that you are living now is past tense, only look and work toward your manifested desires, your dreams, always work and look to the future, don't look at past tense that is old news and you keep on perpetuating it, but some past tense situations are a good platform to re-discover a feeling of which you want to feel, and to remember how it felt, to either re-create it or to let it go.

We are all here to live our imaginative dreams; we are all here to bring the dreams into full manifestations. If these dreams we all have were not within us, we would not have a way to our future, and if you keep looking at where you are and behind you, you can't see what is ahead of you.

Many individuals will have many thoughts, and may say a lot from these written words, always before you speak, think about how it feels, this is the only true indicator and guidance that can ever be experienced, if it feels off don't do it, your Source inside does not agree with those thoughts and will not follow you, that is why you feel the off-ness, it is you separating from you. If it feels good, the Source within, always goes with those feelings, which is why it feels good to you.

I had been asking for how to begin speaking in my imagination of speaking to the masses, when all of a sudden an emotional thought came that was so powerfully focused upon how to begin the environment of speaking, I was so lined up and it was so inspiring that sleep did not come to me until the wee hours, and I was so refreshed with little sleep and still swam my lengths the next day, this is when you are powerfully connected to your Inner Being, tiredness is not part of your vibration. This is how the inspiration comes to you. Then to further manifestations when I had been asking for a solution to an outcome to take another direction until my book was excepted into beingness, but nothing felt inspired, it felt like a means to an end, and I was asking for the solution and I felt it was going to be Wednesday and the solution came in by an unlikely source on Wednesday, an indigenous lady came into the voluntary organisation I help in which I had met her just the week before, she said 'I wanted to see you aunty', I just knew a powerful message was coming to me for me, I asked 'Why do you call me aunty', she said 'We are all one, and that you are powerful', and then she said 'You have the voice'. This message was so powerful; I had just received my message to trust in my path.

I had a feeling I was going to meet someone this day, the process unfolded at the voluntary organisation I volunteer at, some books came in on how to speak the

Polish language which I thought I could learn, me being part Polish, but gave it a miss and then within minutes, I served this man in the shop, and he was involved with the Polish and Ukraine upheaval we spoke in depth, but to cut a long story short I rendezvoused with the thought I had which is the magnificent manifestation, the Polish books led to the Polish humanitarian, which was the by-product of the thought and these thoughts were coming into actual manifestations, this is the opening alignment to my Inner Being, when you are aligned more thoughts lead to more manifestations and with this alignment it begins the full blown manifestations of which you have accumulated into your vibration and I just knew the process was happening.

I placed out to the universe an answer to my readiness, a sign to be for a bird to hit my window, of which has never happened, sounds cruel to the bird, but it was a major sign I asked for. The next day, while critiquing my book two birds flew into my window landed on the ledge and chirped and sang and chirped and sang. This has never happened before or since.

I became so vibrationally compatible within that the physical manifestation that I knew in 2007 which was relayed to me must come to me because it is expected, and it is the next logical step for me. While I was in Nelson desperate and needing help as I was being bullied by lawyers to sign away everything, while documents were being drawn I went to a person's house that I knew off who is an accountant and a clairvoyant for guidance. He said get yourself of this document, and then he looked up and said, 'You are going to win lotto buy the ticket' Every time I saw him he would smile and say 'Have you won'.

Nothing happened and this is why so many people leave the flow of the path, you have to find the vibrational energy and I knew it was coming but never knew when or how much, and the way you think it would come, or in which order. It is the unfolding of the story in your imagination is the journey to the manifestation. It is following the clues, the rendezvous that the cooperative components are lighting the way, it is believing and trusting in the process, and most of all it is in how you feel when the clues are given, and this process became the manifested realisation into my vibration.

I came into more emotional feelings that became more thoughts; if conceivable, if we are streams of energy, and if we were to think of streams of energy percolating and forming to a greater mass of energy, and if it is unexplainable but it were true, if we were to begin to bring our mind to a different way of thinking, and we could do this by changing our thoughts of what we are, our stream of energy will become powerful and will expand and grow, so the more that is gathered the more it becomes, this energy becomes a massive powerful energy liken to the sun, it only becomes depleted when you doubt or put fear into the energy sun, when this occurs the sun sends out fire balls and releases all the good purity of energy out. When this occurs it is to refill the sun over and over again and harmonise with what you want, without any doubt, without and fear, without any revenge, without any negative thoughts, without any sadness, without any resistant thoughts, to positive thoughts, to thinking vibrational energy, to think intentional pure thoughts, to having fun, to trust in this powerful stream, until such harmony occurs, to know it just Is, this is where it all begins.

I used to have a saying 'I feel we are puppets on a string and the universe is just playing games with us,' and this feeling was very prevalent, until I experienced and discovered and expanded more, is when I saw who we really are, we really are not the shell of what we have taken on the puppet, but the energy, and this energy is only focusing upon the puppet strings and feeling the vibrational wave vibrating on the strings and not the puppet, and until this focus and magnification of the alignment with the universal Source who is focusing upon the strings is felt, you will forever be dangling out of control and going crazy in all directions, but when the focus comes into being you will have coordination of the strings, and the ease and flow begins, this begins the dance of life, this is the dance that we all have come to enjoy. It is just a matter of turning all that you have been told what you must do, and not do, and who you are meant to be, this is wrong, this is right, really! They have no idea who or what they are, and until then, let go of their own trappings and find you.

The reality of any condition is only a reality; it is the connection to the unseen universal powers is where it is all at. Isn't it conceivable that everyone has created a thought pattern that is so disconnected to who they all are, when you feel yourself being disconnected, re-read, these written words will bring you into alignment.

Joy

*A thing of beauty is a joy forever: its loveliness increases;
it will never pass into nothingness*

: John Keats

The most sort after and asked question is 'What is life all about?' Life is the joyous creation of life.

Joy is living joyful in everyday situations. Joy increases this vibration of energy that resides within us all. Joy makes you glow. Joy is the direct communication with God or with your Inner Being, or your Higher Self, it is being tuned into your Source energy.

Understanding that joy for the most part is no easy feat, more so if situations are not to your liking. It takes incredible discernment to focus on the goal post and to stay vibrational within Self.

Joy gives the impression of running around in joy all day. Joy comes in many different forms, joy can be inspired to an idea, joy can be observing nature and feeling the bliss of the observation within, joy can be in quiet times, joy can be taking time out for oneself, joy can be listening to music, joy can be writing, painting, singing, joy is feeling the pleasure within, the list of joy is endless, this is joy.

It takes a deep knowing and understanding of the laws of the Universe and that law is; you only get what you want, or what you are putting your attention onto into your vibrational escrow, no exceptions.

Joy is the pleasure of your connection with your Source, when in joy the pleasure of life unfolds. It is this deep abiding connection to which you really are; it is the guiding path that directs you to your desires.

Joy increases incrementally to your purpose and to those desires, and outcomes.

Joy is the complete of who you are in this life time, seeking joy in all that is or to become, no matter what the current situation is, it is making the best of what is and look at the good points and build joy and appreciation to the good points, and feel how the emotional vibration shifts, the more you see good the greater the vibration, and the quicker to the realisation of your desires.

This growth is the expansion of your own energy, with each process that you experience, creates an expansion of energy which harmonises with your Inner Being.

Joy is the realisation that any experience is for the greater expansion of who you are in connection to your Source. Every experience is an unfolding of your expansion. Discernment is the knowing that the experience is for a reason, discernment is looking at the experience and evaluating what is it that you are experiencing, this is looking at the why, and then evaluating the process to an outcome of how you emotionally felt to that experience. It is as simple as looking at a situation that is not entirely to your liking, say to a partner where this partner makes you feel miserable, first step is the partner cannot make you feel miserable, only you can make you miserable, no one can make you feel the way you feel, you hold the emotional feelings to your thoughts, look at a different angle of the partner, look at the positive aspects of this partner, begin to build up a joy to the side of the partner that brings out the best in you, to be on a spiritual energy vibrational wave you both have to feel that same vibration, and then the joy is unsurmountable. That is the sharing of the joy, the experience for the both of your Source expansions. When the joy is depleted in the union of a partnership, the Source within realises that the expansion for your growth is not expanding, more so if your attention is for wanting to be more, and the more you focus on what you want the more it will become, the wanted or unwanted.

Source is forever supporting and expanding at all times, you have the choice in to what expansion of which you are wanting to experience.

It is easier to create a thought pattern of the pattern of your partner, my partner is miserable and my partner reflects its misery onto me and to others, my partner wants me to bring my joyous vibrations down to their level, to make them feel better, that sounds pretty screwy that I should have to come down to their level to only make them feel better. I will instead tend to my own vibration and if I feel good maybe it will reflect back to them, and if it does not reflect back to them that is okay, I will tend to my own vibration, for it is in all about how I feel, it is about my appreciation, my alignment, my experience, my joyous time with who I am and who I want to become, that feels a better thought and feeling than tending to someone else's vibration. I now know that it is their vibration and their connection with their Source, and they have the ability to tend to their own vibrational energy and experience a better well-being.

Tending to your own vibration will gather momentum and point you into a direction for the betterment of you, and your own expansion to your Source.

Evidence of Joy
In Physical Vibration

Slumber not in the tents of your fathers! The world is advancing. Advance with it!

:Mazzini

Joy surrounds consistently every day, it reflects through nature, see how nature dances around and provide stimulating experiences, it can be as simple as a butterfly giving you its undivided attention, nature can provide evidence of your thoughts by the simple act of a butterfly tending to match into your vibration, showing you evidence, this way - this way, you are pointing in the right direction, this way - this way, are you the observer of this evidence. Nature plays powerful affirmations, by way of songs, in clouds, by the way you feel, by your thoughts and what thought that is in thought to a question or outcome, have you experienced when you think about someone and suddenly they are there, or have you experienced thinking about someone and the phone rings and it is the very person you were thinking about, have you experienced you saw someone in your peripheral vision and no one was there, have you felt the inclination to do something and you were compelled to do it, have you read or seen something and you resonated with it so profoundly and wild horses would not stop you from doing what was so compelling, have you experienced inner eye vision, have you experienced out of body experiences, have you had thoughts that opened up to more thoughts and you were off and running, have you experienced a voice within and heard it, have you experienced goose bumps, these are all connection to the energy stream of your Inner Being, and this list is endless; are you in tune!

I have incorporated some of my observational evidence as a point of reference for what you can do yourself.

Merlin and the clouds

One night as I was saying good bye to the platform medium speaker outside, the person who was giving the platform medium speaker a lift, had a little dog in the car called Merlin.

I was observing the full moon with one cloud in the clear night sky, and I saw an Irish Setter and a Scotch Terrier in the cloud formation, the Irish setter was full of authority, like follow me with the Scotch terrier in tow, this was the only cloud in the night sky.

The next day I rang a friend, to find out in great tears her dog died yesterday. And Yes! it was an Irish Setter, and then I told her there was a Scotch Terrier in the clouds as well, she said when the Irish Setter was a puppy its best friend was a Scotch Terrier, and then to top it all off, the dog in the car was called Merlin, the infinite intelligence master guide that my friend works through is called - 'Merlin'. For my friend this was such a joy to know her pet was acknowledged, and more so by infinite intelligence.

My Dog

While walking along the beach, I saw in the clouds a cloud formation of a Bichon, "Olly Hi!" I said - this is my dog in spirit - next minute two ladies were walking their Bichon along the beach, the Bichon came bounding towards me.

The ladies called out "Olly come" I knew then without a doubt the universe was Confirming my path. How many dogs cross your path with the identical name that is out of the ordinary.

Feathers and number plates

I had this deep feeling my lawyer was letting me down.

Feeling absolutely devastated and having to make a trip to Whakatane.

Going down stairs into the garage, and to see my whole garage floor was covered in grey feathers floating everywhere, my first thought was I am being let down, fuming with the higher powers, how you could lead me down this path, and let me down, this was the last straw. (Grey feathers is a sign for me something is happening, or about to, black feathers is absolutely not good, and white is of the highest elevation, this is my emotional feeling outcome of feathers and its colours)

I am not in a good place, feeling so let down, so hurt to be led down a dead end path, while driving observing, and not in a good space, I was waiting at the traffic lights, when a car in the right lanes number plate said 'Defiant' and the car in the left lane said 'Lawgirl' the message was coming through to me to be defiant and be the law girl, you can do it. As soon as I returned home I emailed the court registrar and started another process that was being ignored by my lawyer. I then proceeded to place the plaintiff's lawyer into the civil court for Fiduciary duty of care and working in conflict. 'Defiant Law Girl'. Inspired observational messages are everywhere.

I was swimming one day and in my lane I thought I had a bug floating ahead, when I came up the object it was a grey feather floating in my lane, I just knew it was not time yet! Out of all the lanes it was in my lane only, non-physical always interacts, if you observe.

Black Feather

Feathers were a significant sign for me, this day I decided not to walk as I was over having the black feather crossing my path, I went to work the next day and in the hallway was a large black feather, there is no way even conceivable that a feather could be in this hall way, the joke was on me to avoid something, another way round will be found to deliver the message.

Songs

My flat mate said to me " How could you tell what they were up to" I said "It is in the eyes" a song came on the radio as soon as I said this, 'A Thousand eyes tell a thousand lies' we were both overcome with goose bumps, which is another confirmation sign.

Radio

While driving to work, I saw three cars in succession with the number plate XB, I knew what XB meant to me, I asked the universe "If this is what I think it is please show me a sign", within seconds the radio announcer said "Has everyone got their X Boxes yet?" Wow!

My friend and one of her signs

My friend had been waiting to hear if she was to get this contract awarded to her. On this day she observed a few number plates 'CHQ' followed by a few 'BNZ'.

At home, the answer on her answer machine was, "We have given you the contract, and have sent the cheque in the mail" she rang with excitement about her messages, and now we are waiting in anticipation for the cheque to see if it is what we think; you guessed it, it was a 'BNZ CHQ'.

Courier vans

Traveling home one day I saw at least eight courier vans all within one block, I asked the universe, "Is this a message for me, am I going to receive a courier parcel" I got 'No' by way of feeling. When I arrived home, at my front door was a courier parcel, confirmation of the courier vans were being projected to me, the parcel was not for me, but my neighbor.

Being an observer is a powerful confirmation that you are on the right path and that you are never alone.

Powerful delivery

In January 2012 I went to the post shop, and the lady at the counter, with full of animation and expression quite out of the ordinary said "And you have a lovely day" I looked at her and said "Is something special on today" " No but you have a lovely day" the - you - was so vocalized, I just knew there was a message in this, as I was walking home a seagull came straight at me of attack, squawking away, I thought am I being gull able or is this bringing in laughter! Not sure, as I crossed the street into my driveway, I saw a courier van coming along the road, I just knew deep within me that this van was going to go into my driveway, which it did, no parcel for me, but I had this deep inner knowing that a large parcel or package was coming my way, I opened the door to my home, and the phone was ringing, it was my daughter in Australia, I started relaying the messages, when I finished relaying what had happened my daughter turned around and said "How would you like to come over, we have a tax refund and are paying for you to come over" I was gobsmaked, and more so, the messages were given all within minutes. See how this works, this is the power of reading into situations that come out of the ordinary and being open to all that is around.

Raining money

On Christmas day while driving, I asked infinite intelligence 'When is the money going to rain on me' promptly a ten dollar note flew over my windscreen while I was driving; I certainly received what I asked for. Be aware of the choice of words used.

Black Crows

Taking a breather on a seat gathering my breath while walking up a hill, and thinking about this person I was to maybe form a relationship with, a black crow kept on flying around me, my first thought was an omen, but being of pureness I disregarded this thought, this was the first time I have ever encountered a black crow on my walk which places relevance onto the situation, the next day we went to a beach for the day, and out of the blue two black crows came down and stayed with us, and all I could think was is this a good sign or bad. Then out of the blue my parents turned up for the week, and then a few other small things that curtailed us meeting up again, these are all the signs the universe is saying NO! Then I received in thought a song 'True colours that's why I love you' I decided to end this relationship well as you can gather his true colours came into being. The moral of the story is, always trust your first intuitive thought, and take notice of the signs.

Crystal Clear

In my third eye vision I was given a clear vison of crystal clear water and I was basking in the beauty of the clear water and the sand, then I was being scratched by crystals that I came upon, the crystals were significant to make me understand the vision, that being (crystal clear) I was relating the vision to my daughter when the weather reporter on TV at the same time said 'It is going to be a crystal clear day', this is how infinite intelligence confirms to you when you are on the same vibrational path. When this clarity was confirmed my whole being just evolved into a greater awareness and expansion and everything just became so crystal clear.

Behind closed doors

I was talking to a friend about a situation, and she said "You do not know what happens behind closed doors". When I was of the phone, I sat down and asked my guides "If what was said is true please show me a sign" was I so wrong in what I saw and felt?

Within seconds the radio was playing the song, "You don't know what happens behind closed doors".

Passport

Intuitively I kept on getting an inner thought all day "Get your passport" I had wanted to change my passport back to my maiden name, but I was not financially able too. Finally, I listened to this thought and applied for the papers to be sent. A few days later they arrived, and I did say to infinite intelligence "Are you happy now it is here" perusing through the fine print I was completely gobsmacked! it said if you have two years left on your passport and you have been divorced within the year the passport can be changed free of charge, I fitted all these categories. The moral of the story listen to that inner voice that keeps on giving you the thought, and act upon it, it just may surprise you.

A Peg

My daughter wanted a peg for her bird cage, one that clips; she put the thought out in the universe, the next day while walking up the hill there was a peg waiting for her. This is being non-resistant in thought and the universe came and manifested her thought. The universe loves to play and most of all to show you they are hearing you.

Daughter and fifty dollar note

My daughter needed fifty dollars, and had no funds to take out the fifty dollars at the supermarket, it was significant for her as she decided to have a life changing direction for her and the children, while walking past the shopping trolleys and me pushing the trolley, I saw a fifty dollar note on the ground, and all I could say to her was 'pick it up, pick it up' and all she could say was 'Oh! My God, Oh! My God', without me realising the significance of it all, being the fifty dollars and wanting this amount and what it was for, the universe works heaven and earth for you when the timing is right.

Gluteus maximus

Manifestations come in many forms as simple as my grandchild, all of seven years old, asking me about gluteus maximus, why this was so wonderful is that, while I was swimming my lengths, I kept on getting gluteus maximus, and I was thinking was there something wrong or work the muscle more , but what it was, was the universal energies relaying a thought form word that I will hear again, and by a very unlikely source of my seven year old grandchild, when you are connected to this life stream you then understand it was a message for either keep on going or we are acknowledging you, but for so many they disregard such incredible information coming to them, and they say it is just a coincidence, nothing is a coincidence, just wake up and begin to observe.

Birds flying into my window

I placed out to the universe an answer to my readiness, a sign to be for a bird to hit my window, of which has never happened, sounds cruel to the bird, but it was a major sign I asked for. The next day, while critiquing my book two birds flew into my window landed on the ledge and chirped and sang and chirped and sang. This has never happened before.

Hawk flying into my window

I wanted a punctuation to my thoughts, and I wanted it big, as I was biking to my daily swim, I gave thought to a punctuation when I looked up in the sky and saw a Hawk and thought now that would be a punctuation. The next day I was at my computer when all of a sudden, I heard a noise and low and behold a Hawk flew into my window, the feather dust is still on the window pane and I treasure and look at this sign with great joy.

Burkes Pass

I was talking with my daughter about a lake in the South Island of New Zealand, and that it was behind Lake Tekapo, my daughter was googling the lake when her phone rang and it was her father and he was relating to her about an accident at Burkes Pass, and I said 'That is how you get to the lake' this was unrelated to our topic but so incredibly related to how the Universe works and communicates to you and through all means, and the clarifying moment was did you get the message and believe in us.

How joyous can this be, that nature is a vibration and interacts with us, that there is an undisputed non-physical infinite intelligence energy guiding each and every one of us with this powerful energy, be an observer, and you will never be alone or lost.

Joy becomes your friend, your lover, your wants, your desires. To be in tune with joy creates expansion of joy, which creates the deliverance of what you are wanting. Joy is the unfolding guiding point of pointing in the right direction. Joy is the all-knowing that all is well, joy expands your Source to an even greater expansion, and this joyous expansion is felt by non-physical infinite intelligence, and with this joyous vibration then becomes manifest able desires. Joy is the appreciation of life, the appreciation of where you are at, in any point in time, no matter what the condition is right here right now.

Joy allows the unfolding; joy is the unfolding. Joy is in the knowing of the laws of the universe, and the relationship of where you are in vibration.

Joy is the all-knowing that you know, and the allowance is allowing the laws of the universe to deliver in perfect timing.

Many persons have clear seeing via the third eye known as the pituitary gland, in the inner vision you have access to symbols, numbers, words, pictures that are relevant to you, and with the relevance of these images you have a deep knowing what is being portrayed to you. You may have clear seeing of flashes of light, orbs and objects that come through in your periphery vision, you see something moving and once you focus onto what you are observing it disappears, the periphery vision is the lazy focus unhindered with obstacles and is a clear way of seeing infinite intelligence. You may be able to feel feathers tickling your face or part of your body when you are meditating, when you are in no resistance, or you may be able to smell smells related to a past entity that is letting you know they are surrounding you. You may be able to audibly hear clearly words, or have thoughts down loaded into clear knowing. Messages are relayed through symbolically; it is for you to understand the symbol or feel what the symbol meant.

We may have one or some of these resources; sometimes the resources are brought forward for you to believe and have focus and for you to believe all things are possible.

The focus is to believe, and once you believe and are willing, all you have to do is ask, the resources that come forward is unsurmountable, trust and believe and have complete faith, and your life will never be the same again.

I began to see in my vision of the third eye the pituitary gland after my near death experience, it was a time when I was in great need of help, this is when the resources came through to guide me along the way, I could also feel the physical touch of feathers, and I could smell smells. I also see clearly orbs, flashes of light and feel this strong energy within me. At one time all these resources were very strong, until I reached the stage of further advancement for my expansion growth, it began the growth of thought and how thought is an energy, and then how the emotions and feelings are the indicators of where you are taking momentum too. Once again you are Source energy and are an extension of Source you are here on the leading edge of thought, right here right now on new thought, there is nothing more leading edge than the thought you are focusing on, this is how the Source and infinite intelligence expands with your thoughts, these are thoughts that are all accumulated into this life time reality, not just your thoughts but all thoughts, every existence of all thoughts working on the leading edge of the now, and expanding you into a more fuller you. I have incorporated some of my visions to help gather momentum for you to focus, as what I can do, you can do as well.

Surgery and grandchild

My youngest daughter was due to have a baby at the end of June 2008, I was scheduled for surgery to have my nose reconstructed, after the accident as the first surgery did not work, this was for the 9th of June, before this date, I kept on getting the queens crown, and a number nine in my psychic vision, to me I thought it was to do with a court document as this is the court crown seal, to decipher or interpret the message, sometimes it can be a bit frustrating, because we are not aware of what the message is, only that it is given to you for a reason and in metaphoric symbols.

The message was to let me know my granddaughter was going to be born on the ninth, and the ninth was the queen's birthday in New Zealand, hence the queens crown.

The night before surgery I was helping my daughter with her labour pains with reiki, she had been in labour for three days on and off, Her partner and I felt something was wrong, they went into hospital, and I tried to get some sleep at four in the morning, I was scheduled for surgery at eight am, I was totally dehydrated from abstaining from no fluids all night, pre- surgery, and shattered.

In recovery I found out that my daughter may have to have a caesarian, I could not believe it, here I was stuck in a private hospital, and could not do a thing. My daughter in the meantime had turned the baby herself, and had her water birth that she had wanted, and all of this was unbeknown to me.

The nurses in my hospital were all waiting, like me to find out, what, or when the baby was arriving, we even were making predictions of the time of arrival between all of us.

When I was taken to my room I went into deep meditation, I was taken to places I did not know existed, other planets, and incredible visions.

I was then given the number twenty eight, and then the number seventy eight flew straight towards me in my vision, I wrote this on the hospital writing pad, as I felt this was significant but not knowing why.

In my third eye vision I was given a baby fetus, with hands and toes that were so prominent, then suddenly I saw bubbles, this was the water birth, and a tube canal, I knew then, that this was my grandchild being born, I looked at the clock and it said ten fifteen and then I was given the name of my grandchild floating in my vision everywhere, I knew then, that, she was born, the next message that was given loud and clear through clairaudient (hearing) was "Messiah".

Unbeknown to me, I thought my daughter was having a caesarian, I had no idea that she was having a water birth hence the bubbles, and the numbers in my vision 28: 2+8=10 and 78: 7+8=15. I was given the time of the birth which was 10.15 when my grandchild's head emerged.

Why was I given Messiah, was it the Messiah with me, or is my grandchild going to do incredible works, we will just have to see.

My grandchild is three, and her mother had her choose the colours for the Christmas cards to be made to send to everyone, and this child chose colours for each family member, that represented and portrayed each of the members, and for me she chose white, this is purity, later on my granddaughter had to choose again a colour of a birthday card for me, and she chose white again, my daughter said this is for nanas birthday, not for Christmas, for my granddaughter to promptly say "Nana is always white" the connection she and I have is beautiful.

Albert Einstein

Albert Einstein was my first clear vision I saw through my third eye, it was absolutely wondrous to have his powerful intelligence in my vibration.

Leonardo d Vinci

I kept on getting in my clairvoyant vision a big nose for three nights and not knowing why.

On the fourth night the face came straight at me, I was so startled I jumped.

I went to a café the next day and saw this person's image on the café wall, I was blown away; I kept on staring at the face.

That night I saw an invite card with this face on it at my daughter's place,

"What is this?" I asked her.

"We have a free pass to Leonardo d Vince at the museum".

"This person came to me, I have to go to it," not knowing why I just got his face.

Leonardo d Vince used his inspirations of design with wood, and I at that time was a wood artist, was this message given to believe in the outer universe, you are on the right path. Keep going.

Warner Brothers

My first ever vision that really sent me into a spin, I was given a Warner Brothers symbol before I could say the word Warner Brothers a name came to me so strong with the same initials W B, in the morning I kept on saying, I know that name, where do I know that name, I went to my index card folder and found the name, not knowing why I was given that name, this happened on the 12th of June 2007. On the 18th the phone rang I answered, and he said this is W B, I near had kittens, and was completely blown away. This person has never phoned me before.

Registered letter and post office key

One night I said to spirit world, leave me alone I want to sleep; a word came through very strong 'Registered Letter'. The next day in my post office box was a registered letter card, I near flipped

Leather Smell

Half in my sleep I asked when is the legal system going to be over. I got a strong scent of leather it was so powerful I had to put my nose into the pillow; this told me that the legal system in the spiritual realm was working very strongly.

Lawyer invoice

May 2008 during the meditation I received these wonderful golden hands this intense feeling inside of me was so powerful, this hand came down and I saw my lady lawyer and her law office team in the telephone book advertising ad, this golden hand came down and pulled her out, the message was loud and clear "It is in God's hands" This was so powerful I felt this intense wonderful glow. Reason for this vision was the next day a letter arrived with her putting me before the debt agency; here I go again defending the reasons for why this account was in-dispute. I put her into the law society for such misrepresentation, as some of the lawyers did say I was totally shafted.

What was amazing was the vision, and to trust that it was, and is, as relayed to me at that time in God's hands, do your paper work and just trust, and it did disappear into the universe's hands.

Radio waves

I received a message for my nephew, which meant nothing to me but was to be revealed to me a few months later.

I received through clairaudient hearing 'Radio waves, music', and feelings of something to do with connecting to the universe. He applied to enlist into the army as a systems communications engineer. Wow! I can do it, get rid of the clutter in your head, and messages come in, thick and fast.

Play boy symbol

While having lunch at work, quietly waiting I saw the playboy symbol vibrating in front of me on the wall, "Why are you giving me this sign" not knowing why, on my way home the news man on the radio said "Madge Simpsons from the Simpsons was going to be on the front cover of the playboy magazine" Well! I cracked up laughing, talk about keeping my faith up!

Police cars

In my third eye vision I was given two police car lights. On my way to work on a Sunday at 6.30am running late, I remembered this vision and thought I had better take notice of this, as I had received a speeding ticket before, and I was given a message it meant nothing to me at that time.

I was given a spiritualist name 'Uri Geller; from overseas, he is renowned for his ability on radio waves, trying to decipher why I was given this name. I was targeted by a speed camera, now I know radio waves! And what it meant. So this time I decided to be aware, just as I was approaching the last stretch of road to work and thinking well it must have been a different meaning, low and behold! Two police cars pulled out of a side street just before work.

Stand tall in what you know

I received a Giraffe in my vision, and I got the words 'Stand tall in what you know'

Timing

I was busy talking to my guides on a walkway, when I got 'Timing' and a strong pulling on my head to look down, beside the walkway was a school bag in amongst the reeds, this school bag had pictures of clocks on it.

Rosemary

During meditation I had a rosemary bush in my vision, wondering why this was given to me. I was about to start a new job the next day, my trainers name for this job was Rosemary.

CD Susan Boyle

In meditation I kept on getting Susan Boyle, the next day on my birthday I received a Susan Boyle CD.

$ and M

25 October 2012 I received a $ sign M – Money then a man in a black coat and top hat carrying a briefcase, came forward to me, snow was everywhere, he sat on the park bench and all I was focusing on was the snow-ice on the chair, the message I felt the money is on a freeze.

Coffee Cup

A coffee cup was revealed to me in my third eye vision one morning, within one hour I receive a telephone call to go and have coffee. Universal energies do like to play.

Runny Eyes

At one stage during my marriage, while in sleep, I had an incredible pouring of tears, yet I was not crying, my eyes were overflowing, it was quite bizarre. This was about six months before the accident, I know at that stage I was thinking 'Was this all my life', like a mid-life crisis. I would wake up many times to this great flood pouring out of my eyes. A friend of mine is having the same experience, she is going through great spiritual upheaval, and she could not understand where all this was coming from, she felt she was not crying, just like me. I was able to relate to her, I read somewhere in a spiritual book, it is the soul cleansing itself with-out pouring, it is the release of resistance. It is washing the spiritual eyes. I could relate to this totally, and to relate this to her was a comfort, for she understood.

Since my situation changed, I have not had the pouring eyes again.

Thoughts

20 April 2013 I received a message 'Letting go of detachments' in thought I asked 'what detachments' received 'Thoughts' then I was in a black four wheel drive trying to pass trucks (new) down a rough mountain- then I ran onto a big black crystal rock (snowflake obsidian) which gave way but I landed gently then I got a huge concrete cut polished wall. The message for me I felt was a rough time coming, snowflake obsidian is very highly spiritual and a concrete wall – enough for now. I felt all these visions; it is a feeling that you know what the meanings are to the visions.

Verbatim

'Verbatim' came booming through my clairaudient hearing while meditating, this was when I was putting all the legal documents together for the court. The universe wanted me to put everything in word for word.

To further encapsulate this, my friend who was staying with me teaching me the art of connecting, she was looking through a second hand shop flicking through books, when a piece of paper flew out, what a shock for her to see, it was a piece of a dictionary, and with the very word 'Verbatim'

My Near Death Experience

My life was in turmoil with the disintegration of family and marriage, looking for a solution, while driving quietly in thought a clairaudient voice said to me 'There is going to be an accident' I had no idea where or what, when out of the blue this car came straight for me on the wrong side of the road. How can a voice a minute before my accident tell me there was going to be an accident? Where did this come from? I started to question I wanted answers, to this unseen non-physical universe; there is something greater here than any physical being can begin to understand. This was my turning point into the discovery of the unseen world; this began the direction of my passion and purpose.

CDW731

The ambulance that took me to the hospital nearly stretched my youngest daughter, she being very intuitive saw the number plate on the ambulance, which was her initials and birth date when you add the numbers it equals 11 which is her birth date, at the same time she had been receiving a lot of ambulance number plates which were significant to her as they related to a few people that she knew had been in accidents.

Energies

I was watching my cat sitting and preening his paw, when all of a sudden I saw this energy run right past him to the dining room table, about the size of a small cat or rat, when I saw this at the same time my cat swung his head so fast and was watching the very same thing I was observing. Now that is the ultimate confirmation of what I saw my cat saw. He watched it for a short while and went back to preening.

I was watching my cat once again preening, when he had finished he got up and walked away and I was amazed to see his energy glowing where he had laid and then I saw the energy of his track where he walked away, I was in a non-resistant place to see this vision, until I came into focus and then the vision was lost.

I consistently see energies around everyone and everything, I can pick up the energy of the TV program and put it onto the wall and bring the whole picture into view on the wall. I can view a person and when they move I still see the energy of where they were.

Orbs

Energies of orbs are everywhere, normally these can be observed in you periphery vision, this is the lazy focus that is unhindered with direct viewing, we all get these flashes of something or seeing something that is not their but you know you saw something, orbs usually show up in white circles or shapes in your photos, and they are usually disregarded as a mark, when you observe closely you can see faces and signs. My nephew was being inducted into the army, and I took a few photos, all the photos were orb less until the last one this was the signing of the papers, the whole photo was full of orbs, what was interesting there were two orbs next to two other recruits that had a orb circle next to them and an arrow inside of them pointing to them, I wander what they were trying to say!

Orbs viewed with a partner

While basking in bed in the early morning, and observing the ceiling I saw a few orbs, I said to my partner can you see what I am seeing the lights of orbs, for him to point out them as well as more, and then the whole ceiling was glowing orbs in profusion, it was incredible and even more, is that he saw them and that the energies were so incredibly high that the universe was making a full display for us.

It is time to settle

I asked the universe for a sign if this person is the person for me, and I asked for a sign, as I crossed the road, the turning sign in the middle of the road had a sticker on it which said ' it is time to settle' it was the nationality sign for this persons nationality, I had two fleeting thoughts, is it time to end or to increase my thoughts into settling, I allowed a few days for an outcome to this message and it came, and the message was to forget and move on it certainly was time to settle this thought pattern and when I came to this thought, I was joyous, and also I felt it is time for me to settle it.

Boswellia

I was woken up one night to a booming voice 'Boswellia' I thought I know that name why am I getting this, I wrote it down and looked up on the internet in the morning, Boswellia is Frankincense and it is a powerful herb for the use of arthritis, 'Wow' a powerful delivery for a cure for my knees. Since this message I used the Boswellia which released the resistance of the condition, and then I began to focus upon the vibration of wellness, now my knees are more vibrationally youthful.

Glimpses of a friend with arthritis

While meditating I received an image of my friend who has severe arthritis, what I observed in my inner vision was my friend in total wellness, it was a beautiful sight to behold, I knew within my inner vision that the wellness is in the taking for everyone, and that wellness abounds all, it is letting go of the resistant thoughts to allow the wellness in, and the glimpse of this vision showed me total wellness.

My in-laws

In my vision while meditating I received a vision of my in-laws glowing in happiness and young and vibrant going into a restaurant with a lot of glowing light in the vision, without realising that it was the same week that my father in-law passed away some years ago, their favorite past time was eating out, and the vison came to me as there was a great love between us, even though I was estranged from the son.

Insight

I was thinking about my book 'Clarity' and I was wanting to add into the chapters and giving thought which turned to feeling good. While I was biking, I felt a feeling to look up on the other side of the road when a car went past and had panel writing 'Insight' I had the insight confirmed.

Thought form

While at the swimming pool a discussion was occurring between a few people and myself and with the life guard about how they have to deal with altercations at the pool and the swimming lanes, now this energy thought vibration was forming at the pool, so much so that the next day my friend and I were trying to sort out which lane to use as a lot of slow swimmers were in the lanes as well as walkers, we asked the life guard the same one from the previous day to sort out the lanes, the obvious one was to shift the walker to the walker lane, well as you can gather the vibration of thought was so prevalent from the previous day and reverted to an action energy and of which was not pleasant for anyone or the life guard, but for me I identified the energy and it was a continuation of a vibration from the previous days topic, and this was a clarifying moment, and I knew the universe was providing the evidence of the thought form energy for me to observe.

....

This is only a few snippets of what I have received and how resourceful infinite intelligence is at orchestrating events when you are in the receptive mode.

Miracles

There are two ways to live: you can live as if nothing is a miracle; you can live as if everything is a miracle.

: Albert Einstein

Creating miracles into manifestation is in the capabilities of each, and all, who understand the laws of the universe. Miracles are the natural ability that we all have, and for those that have the miracles call it a miracle, it is better to call it a miracle than to observe that it was your point of attraction of your vibration to create into reality.

It is getting your head around the concept that you are not here in the physical you are here in the spiritual and this is what you have to connect back too, it is a major thought thinking process of changing what you view yourself as, it is listening and feeling for the signs, not observing and making it happen, because normally it does not work out, but the inspired feelings is guiding you to the next path to the next path. Be honest when reading this, have you had these feelings of inspiration, if you are really honest then you will and can relate to this connection. I know you all have had this feeling, and why, because what I can do you can do as well. Being in true alignment is deliberately allowing the next path, all you have to do is put into your imaginative filing system all the things you want, and feel how it feels to have the wants if it came into being, if it feels really good in thought then you are connected to your

Inner Being, if it feels confused or wishy washy it is not it, or you have some vibrational cleaning up to do.

The universal laws are all about emotions, feelings, thoughts, and what vibrational frequency you are on.

Vibration is a fine tuning of your frequency imagination into the law base universe to what you want.

If you want a lover your frequency has to be a match and be in frequency with this vibration.

If you want more money your frequency has to be a match and be in frequency with this vibration.

Everything is energy, everything is vibration, we are here to create; we are here to deliberately create, we are here to remember our own emotional guidance system, we are here to tap into the indicators of this emotional guidance. It is a fine attunement of your Source energy within, to the frequency of non-physical infinite intelligence, once it is a match to that desire and it is felt in deep meaningful vibration, then and only then the miracles will manifest into reality.

It all comes down to where your point of attraction is to the laws of the universe, and that is you only get what you are wanting, no exceptions. You can want a desire, but if the desire has a negative to that desire, this becomes the predominant thought, it is what you are focusing upon is what you will receive, this is the prominent thought base, the not having of it.

What sets you apart from believing, is what has been taught to you, many well-meaning peers, teachers, parents disrupt your progress dictating who you should be or to conform to their ways, when they do not even recognise their own guidance system, or of Source or what Source is, and to what relationship that you have with your own Source.

Disruption of Religion

Religion is the frozen thought of man out of which they build temples.

: Jiddu Krishnamaurti

Vibrational miracles were not only evolved thousands of years ago but are on-going here today, and are disregarded by religious beliefs, they only believe in one man, Jesus who departed a long time ago, the doctrine's idolization of the departed person, separated the individuals, from ever rationalizing the spiritual vibrational expansion of themselves, as being of higher consciousness and that individual man is The Source, individual man is what they call God.

The religions perspective is to let you stand still, morphed in the old ways, which was at a different time thousands of years ago, and has been so indoctrinated and given any credence to the present times, in the right here and now. But religion decreed that Jesus was the only miracle maker, these teachings kept the expansion of the Source the God within to be placed into a catatonic stupor. To teach a habit from the old ways is easier than to believe that we can do and experience in the right now manifestations and vibrational energies, of thought, feelings, emotions, and that these emotional feelings and thought is where it is all happening. You are here at the very core on the leading edge of thought, you are here creating new thought to expand you, and expand the universe. Law of attraction is future tense, not past tense. Expansion is not re-creating history, that is old news, that is old thought, this does not expand The Source (God) but holds The Source (God) unexpansive, we are not unexpansive we are expansion forever expanding.

You are eternal, and re-emerge into the physical at another given point in time to experience for the expansion of your Source your Inner Being, and that the culmination of the older wiser part being the non-physical part of you, has lived many life times with this knowledge, and has the knowledge of this power house of what Source is and can do, and that is, you create your own reality, your own purpose and your own manifestations. You are the extension of Source energy, and most of all you are Source, and to never lose sight of this, you are one whole part of The Source (God) not separate from it. YOU ARE IT, with infinite intelligence the masters, and all of those who have made transition into the non-physical guiding you along the way, cheering you along, with the full knowing what they didn't know in the physical, and now know how easy creating is, and creating your desires and your purpose into reality. This is a pulsating parallel universe, that being the non-physical and the physical, the non-physical is living your desires, and it is you in the physical coming into alignment with the desire that you have projected to the non-physical.

The ministries have been controlling peoples very own guidance system for centuries; they make laws and control other individual's guidance system to conform to their ways. One must only look up to and only love Christ for he is the truth and salvation, and that you are here to serve God, what about your truth, what about the love for oneself. These teachings create, and has created confusion to so many, created a disbelieving vibration, a judgmental vibration, a non-believing of the eternal Source within each and every one of us, and most of all you are not here to serve God, but you are here to expand God, which is you.

The impression of man is that God resides outside of you on a throne and dictates to you, and places fear and damnation, and he is a judgemental God, God is separate from you, God is blamed for so many catastrophic events, this is where the logic of these teachings about God, and to fear God, why does God take the good, and the list is endless.

God does NOT reside on a throne, God does NOT place fear or damnation or judgement on you, only YOU and YOU alone place fear, damnation and judgement on YOU, for you are The Source, you are what religion and man calls God, this entity of God resides within you. Nothing more and nothing less: You are IT. You are all here as unique physical beings and are all here calling yourselves to the well-being and wholeness to whom and what you are.

Jesus was a physical and non-physical entity and was no more special than you, he came forth to experience for his own vibrational energy and for his own expansion of Source, he came forth to create and grow to a higher vibration, he understood he was eternal, and will re-emerge back into the physical at another given point in time, and not only is he eternal, so are you, and you will re-emerge again and again. The creation of the bible exploited Jesus and in turn exploited many, when you can all do what he did, but instead have held Jesus above all else and made him your guidance, and to love him and him only, instead of you loving you and doing the same as he did. You are all of the flow of energy, and this energy flows through you; you are The Source and you are all Gods seeking the joyful vibration of truly being God in all its pureness, and maintaining being the totality of being the willing representative, the willing participator of The Source.

"Is it not written in the scriptures <u>ye are all Gods</u>" Psalm 82.6

"I consecrate myself to meet their need for <u>growth in truth and Holiness</u>, I am not praying for these alone but also for <u>the future believers</u>" John 17: 19-21TLB

Once again you are Source (God), you dictate to you, when this understanding happens, you will create an expansion so powerful within.

"The kingdom of heaven is within" Luke 17-21

'Trust (believe) in the lord <u>your G</u>od' 2Chronnicles 20:20

You have to be tuned into your frequency vibrational energy, and then to acknowledge that there is a greater universal law, the law of being in pure holiness to your Source, this is what you have come into this chosen life time reality to experience the pureness of positive thoughts, that thought is a vibration, that emotions are a vibration, that this is a pulsating vibrational universe.

Isn't it conceivable if God is not separate, but is taught as separate by religions perspective, and if the more is perceived by more that there is no separateness, then what is being taught and created has been misinformed to generations of people, then the religious teachings is coming from a place of being unaware and disconnected to what God is. You cannot teach what you do not know, and to teach what is within in the bible is not knowing God, or this life stream. Isn't it conceivable to teach that God is you, would see the breakdown of these institutions, it is the perpetuating of teaching separateness that is the main stay of all religions.

This life stream of energy does not require temples, to seek solace, for you are the temple, solace is in you, in your thoughts, in your emotions, in your feelings. You are the creator of you, you have come here to experience for the good and holiness of you, you have the vibrational forces within you, you can dream desires, and you can experience natural miracles. It is all about you being in relationship to who you are at any point in time, your relationship with your thoughts, your emotions, your feelings, your mood, and your vibration. This emotional guidance system is always connected to the stream of energy, your emotions are an antenna, and it is consistently turned on; it is just a matter of focusing into the receiving mode.

The quality of your thoughts, and the quality of your match to that desiring thought, and you holding that emotional desire, it then is law, that infinite intelligence non-physical must bring it to you. That my friends, are and is the laws of the universe, in all its pureness readying you to that desire and manifesting it into reality.

Religious teachings, and there are many, have their own connection within their teachings. If your Inner Being has a calling to reside within one of these institutions, feel into your very core how it feels to you, if it gives you joy then go with that, if you do not feel joy look elsewhere.

The bible and all other religious books

The holy bible; it is decreed that God spoke and then this was interpreted into words by man, by many – many- many men all placing their interpretation onto what was received by infinite intelligence, isn't it conceivable that man's interpretation at that time was on a different vibrational time reality over two thousand years ago, and that collection of thought has no relevance in the here and now. The bible at that time was very metaphysical, and taken out of context by man with their own motives, the bible was created at the time when all the relevant persons were on their own vibrational path and interpreting what they were receiving at that time, where man had his own guidance system thousands of years ago. Man created the bible back when there was an archive of donkeys and carts instead of the present conditions here right now, we have completely evolved and expanded since that time, and the reality is the bible has not expanded thought, but has kept all humans trapped in a stuck environment of no thoughts, no emotional feelings, and no trusting in their own guidance system.

You have your own guidance system in this present time reality, we have expanded further with the wisdom and knowledge of thoughts that have accumulated for the past two thousand years, these thoughts have accumulated knowledge and have forever expanded thought, we are forever expanding evolution not standing still, just as we are interpreting our own guidance system, connect to this life time reality, and to indoctrinate your own guidance, for you have come forth to gather your own knowledge. We are all Christ's living in the here and now; you just have forgotten who you really are, you have to discover the very essence of you. You are all Gods and all Christ energy expanding, you can do just as Christ did, and in turn expanding the Universe to even greater thoughts, for the Universe is a pulsating energy of collective consciousness of vibration of thought, each thought is a new thought, all streams of thought is a universal vibration. You are right here in the now on the leading edge of thought, creating new thoughts and expanding those thoughts. Law of attraction is future tense, not past tense. The past tense is only good when you recognise a glimpse in your past that is a match in your vibration right now, it is a good deciphering place to recognise it if it is a wanted or unwanted emotional feeling.

Forgiveness is perpetuated in the teachings, forgiveness is focusing on what went wrong, it is not from a place of who they really are now, and it focuses on negative past tense, instead of looking at the magnificence of where they are now. The secret to forgiveness is blaming someone, and making them the blame, instead of one's own self-empowerment. This forgiveness became a contributor into my experience within my own family, when I was bomb blasted with 'I forgive you' and 'I was thinking for what', it was an issue in them that I had no understanding off because my energy was not tapped into that emotional energy, and I was expected to bow down to something that I was not even aware off. It wasn't until I understood about emotional energies later on that this was their issue and not mine, and it is a forgiveness issue inside oneself to release and let go, not blame another for one's own emotional state.

The bible relates to many negative connotations that incite momentum of negativity and acts of retribution. It is only in the disconnection from them that righteousness in religion that creates the mayhem; it is through this disconnection that those things make sense. This is not The Source (God), The Source (God) does not follow this path, and this is the momentum created by physical beings that were not aligned with The Source (God) within them.

Nobody can convert you if you are in total well-being and being who you really are, covertness can only become, if you are not aligned with who you really are, to be converted is to line up, and be who they want you to be. The only religion is between You and You.

Future believers

There are many-many extremely metaphysical persons living in the here and now who are tuned into The Source energy that far exceeds the bible and any religious organisation, let go of archived past teachings and connect to a far greater intelligence of the universal infinite intelligence, seek these persons they are up-lifters not convertors, tune back into who you really are, and to what you really intended to do before you came into this physical body, you fully intended to experience what you created before you came into this life time reality, you fully intended to have fun along the way, let go of the trappings of the thoughts that don't serve you, let go of the emotions that don't serve you, let go of misguided misaligned teachings and discover this guidance system within you and before you know it the culmination of what you have placed into your vibration will come to you.

Fundamentalists

Fundamentalism is guided by the old theory of thought; this thought does not open up to new ideas, or new thought, or even recognising goodness, peace and feeling good, within themselves or others. This thought has created discord and disconnectedness for many thousands of years; and these conditions have not changed in this form of thought vibration. This thought form is always blaming someone instead of self-empowerment of oneself.

The act of terrorism, is created by individuals so out of synch from who they are, these individuals incite fear as the momentum of what they are creating in their own momentum of thought vibrational path, without realising that they came here as excited beings to create the momentum thoughts of love, feeling good and kindness, are then misguided by individuals who are disconnected and insecure, and out of the vibration of who they are meant to be, and this cycle just is created over and over, without even realising, or knowing, that there is a better way of thought, than what is being created now.

'When you are told: 'Follow what God has revealed,' they reply: 'we will follow what our fathers practised,' even though their fathers understood nothing and had no guidance'. Koran 2:168

'Your God is one God'. Koran 2:163 the word <u>your</u> is taken out of context and distorted of the use of the word <u>your</u> which is a word used to indicate that <u>one belonging to oneself.</u>

The discord is so prevalent and creates more discord and disunity, the disconnection from them and their Source is so powerfully disconnected that they take the least path of resistance, and for these individuals is to release themselves back into the non-physical, and come back and re-create a new way of thought, and expand thought into appreciation, love and harmony, and to remember to feel good about themselves and feel good about others.

It does not matter what religion that has been created in this time or past life experiences, they all have the same principles in goodness, and that is to love, and to be in harmony. What is created from the results of the trauma, is for individuals to look at only what they want, these fundamentalists become great teachers, because through the result of the trauma is born a new thought, to look and resonate to a new idea, and expand new thoughts. This is taking new thought to not look at the dramatic, as these thoughts only create more dramatic, the more you look, the more dramatic it becomes, only look at the harmony. These thoughts come together collectively for greater harmony and understanding. To collectively think only of what you do want, this is the only vibration that is to be attended too, the more you think this vibrational thought the more it becomes, trust in the power of goodness, this is a very powerful energy.

The discorded condition of the result of trauma is for the expansion of you, and all other individuals to ignore this condition, and place the power of thought into harmony, and peace, and to close <u>your own gap</u> through the result of the trauma, if the gap is not closed, the result is the trauma will come to you, is the things you do not want, think only of what you want. Looking at the positive aspect creates energy that is more powerful, than what is happening in a discorded situation, what creates the energy of not powerfulness is doubt, disbelieving and negative attitudes. The news is very good at sending discorded messages; they have great delight in repeating and growing the momentum of disassociated negative proportions, the media is so out of alignment that they want all others to join them, look the other way, and only look for better new ideas of thought. You are not ignoring the condition, it is not putting your head in the sand, or being irresponsible, what you are creating is re-focusing and re-aligning only to better thoughts, and this is the most powerful energy of all, to make changes to any conditions.

Analogy of vibrational expansion; the light bulb

We are forever and eternally receiving and pulsating energy; we come forth by virtue to expand this energy to an even greater level of understanding for our own growth, all of us are on different energy vibrations. We came here as lighted beings into this eternal phase of our life time, full of light and eagerness and then bless our parents, teachers, piers, the list is endless they dimmed this light until a progression of darkness becomes the viewing platform, you catch glimpses of this light, and know there has to be better, there has to be more, then becomes this progression of seeking this yearning to this emotional energy of lightness, it is liken to a light bulb, some of us come back to experience and are running on a small, medium or large wattage, we come forth to build our wattage of thought to the highest wattages of thought vibration, we come forth to create the wattage energy within, to expand this thought wattage, you are not here to diffuse the thought wattage this is not the expansion of who you really are. This wattage is to build the eternal energy of completeness of pureness, pureness of understanding, pureness of understanding contrast, understanding of the emotional indicators, understanding the better you feel is the indicator that you are going the right way, and the eternal source within is showing you more emotional feelings and guidance of elation to this flow, understanding your mood is an emotion, this is the focal point, pointing you in either direction, the better you feel the better it gets, and the better it gets is where everything is, all your dreams, hopes and desires, this is the manifestation platform.

To expand to the level of the highest pureness where the wattage energy is completely at its highest lighted vibration this is where we all want to reside, it is in the pureness of completeness into wholeness of The Source, this is your sole purpose of which you came forth to do, is to expand and remember that you are this energy and are vibrating expansion for your eternal growth, forever changing and expanding and being more.

You are eternal - You are eternal - You are eternal.

You deliberately created you into being.

Your purpose is to deliberately create and deliberately feel manifestations into beingness.

You rise again and again and again and again.

Your experiences are for your expansion.

Your sole purpose is expansion and is to remember and connect to this stream of consciousness.

Your sole purpose is to be joyful.

Your purpose is remembering that joy is where it is all at and begins.

Your purpose is to look at life in a vibrational way.

Your purpose is to feel the vibrational emotions.

Your purpose is to understand the emotions; this is your guidance system.

Your purpose is to reacquaint you with your Inner Being.

What is not achieved in this life time of the reality you will do again and again, forever adopting new experiences until you become in oneness or alignment with this vibrational conscious energy stream which is intertwined pulsating energy that flows from you and through you.

Laws of the Universe
Law of Attracting Alignment

The real voyage of discovery consists not in seeking new landscapes but in having new eyes. Imagination is the eye of the soul

: Joseph Joubert

Alignment is the work of the mind, it is in the thoughts, it is in the feelings, it is in the emotions you feel, it is in the reaching for good thoughts, it is making peace with where you are, it is letting go of resistant thoughts, and the timing is all about alignment, and how aligned and in fullness you are with you.

How simple can it be; at which end of the scale are you standing in, and at what point of attraction are you attracting into relation to what you are right now or want to be. Create the energy you want. Be aware of how you feel.

First step; acknowledge that you have come into this physical body in this life time reality to expand the Source within, your Inner Being. Acknowledge that there is a greater part of you that exists while living in this physical body, acknowledge a greater part of you which is your Inner Being is on an eternal experiencing journey, that you are eternal, you can never die, your physical body dies, the non-physical part of you is eternal, and you will come back into another physical body, at another point in time, to re-experience into another life time reality, to expand for your growth and the expansion of your Source.

This is being in true alignment with the non-physical part of you, your Source energy, you are here in the -NOW- leading thought to an even greater level of expansion of your Source through you, to another contrasting thought through you, and you are ALL on the leading edge of focus of thought, you are all here to take thought to a new level, and to allow the flow of this vibrational energy of this collective consciousness of intertwined energy stream which is flowing energy through you, and receiving energy through you.

You may have heard many times you are here, living here the spirit life living in a human form, this is the most truest concept to understand, it is changing your thoughts of not looking at the tangible but feeling the intangible which is the only existence of you, nothing else exists around you, the only thing that exists is the vibration of your Inner Being and the collective consciousness of this stream of energy. What exists outside of you is only the bouncing of place to decipher what you want for you, it is the choosing place only, and then you imagine what you want for you and what feels good for you, for you to build the energy of what you want to come to you.

This is the full embodiment, of who you really are, an energy stream, to what you want to become, for an even greater experience of expansion of your Inner Being within, and when you do, avenues of thought and feelings begin to emerge, vibrational emotions are felt, these feelings are the indicators; they form impressions, impulses and thoughts of the next path.

True alignment comes forth from the universal non-physical stream of infinite intelligence energies, guiding the lit path; signs emerge into relation to what you desire, from your dominate thought pattern. When you allow in the vibration into receiving, then this vibration translates into thought, or vision, or hearing, or knowing.

How are indicators reflected; the laws of the universe is a vast pulsating vibrational energy stream of infinite intelligence, it feels, it feels emotions, it feels thoughts, when meaningful emotions are reflected, and it becomes the true essence of who you want to become, the universe works alongside you guiding you, giving you the indicators, are you open to view, feel or hear these indicators;

Indicating signs are reflected all around you, by way of songs, if a song is being persistent in thought, look at the song, look at the lyrics, what is non-physical infinite intelligence trying to tell you or guiding you too. A song can play at the very moment you have a thought or question, being in true alignment you will recognise instantly the message relayed to you.

A thought may pop into your head that is a thought completely out of the blue, look at it and observe the message infinite intelligence non-physical is guiding you, 'this way-this way'.

You may have thought patterns of a question, and open a book or paper, and the very topic that were your thoughts, is reflected back to you. Indicators come via number plates, bill boards, TV, radio, the birds and the bees, the clouds, the list is endless. Unusual signs just jump right at you, observe it, follow your instincts, this is a powerful interaction between the greater non-physical part of you and the physical part of you.

When you are tuned into vibration occurrences start to be played out, you are placed at the right time, in the right place to open doors. Or processes are played out to evolve you onto a greater understanding of your expansion of your Source energy, and when aligned with the desires which you have created in imagination the non-physical brings about the manifestations of the desires.

We are all on different paths, we are all expanding at different vibrations, some of us know our path, and some have no idea until they set out some parameters of intentions, wants and desires, then these wants and desires start to expand and change or evolve even greater expansion of wants and desires, until the realisation that these wants and desires can be manifested into reality, and you can do it by what you are thinking, and by what you are feeling. Your mood is the indicator of the emotions you are attracting.

Define those intentions and desires and allow yourself into the fullness of who you really want to be, or to become, it is all about thought, emotions and feelings, and a deep appreciation of the whole of you into well-being. This is the relationship of your emotions and thoughts holding a stable fine attunement to the atmospheric vibration which can be felt; it is the frequency of being on a radio station and wanting another radio station, you have to tune into this station.

Obstacles cross your path to realign and expand the whole of you to a greater expansion, this is a joyous occasion, and it allows you to look at what vibration you have activated, and defining what the contrast was meant to be, any contrast is redefining who you are, and bringing you further clarity to what momentum you are attracting.

You cannot control your surroundings or what is in the world, but you can control your vibration, your feelings and emotions to feel good, to feel your worthiness, to feel your thoughts, and your own alignment between you and you.

The Law of Attraction says; nothing comes without giving your attention to it, and nothing stays without giving your attention to it. Wanted or unwanted, the unwanted becomes a more dominate thought conditional pattern, the more you observe the more that it becomes, humans have a dominate thought pattern of spewing what IS, which than becomes more of what IS, and the desires and dreams for better are outweighed by the negative thoughts of what IS, then the belief of better or what you know within, is doubted, or thoughts of what could be recedes.

The concept of mirroring is a mirror of you, it is observing like upon like, or that is likened to oneself is drawn, situation upon situation, it is observing you in how you are feeling.

The influence to any subject that being health and well-being, relationships, money, environmental occurrences around planet earth, all these occurrences brings about emotional manifestation which you feel, they become more, the more you put thought to it, or speak it, the more it is. Take attention to what is naturally flowing to you, not what is observationally flowing around you.

Manifestation is evidence of alignment whether with the wants or don't wants.

A belief is only a thought you keep thinking, if it feels good than you are in alignment with your Inner Being, if you feel angst or off-ness of not feeling good, it is you separating you from your Inner Being, your Inner Being is not following you on this belief thought, and the way you know, is how you feel. To understand how you know when you are in alignment, remember how you felt when you fell in love, and how alive you felt and how sleep was not important but this feeling of over powering exhilaration, and everything felt so good and alive, this is pure connection to your Inner Being. Now think about when you were depressed and all you wanted to do was sleep, and a feeling of complete off-ness, this is how you feel the emotional indicators, and to sleep when in depression is a good thing because sleep releases the resistance that you are focusing upon, and re-aligns you to your Inner Being to think and feel better.

You create your experiences; and how you want to define those experiences, and it is you who is allowing those experiences to flow more, or to come to the clarity and release those unwanted thoughts. The mirroring effect is clarifying, you observe, you identify what you don't want, and then focus upon what you do want, and work on your imagination into focusing upon what you really do want.

The secret to the clarity is to do only what feels good, if it doesn't feel good, then don't do it!

Source views the world through you and expands through you. You are a representative of this Source vibrational energy stream, a representative of deliberately creating and deliberately manifesting your creations, you are right here, right now at the leading edge of thought. Thought and your emotions is the process how the universe interacts with you, and you must be on that vibration for the universe to deliver your desires into manifestations, and there is nothing more satisfying and more fulfilling and more exciting than to being a deliberate creator.

Being a Conscious Deliberate Creator or Being the Default Creator

A conscious deliberate creator is aware of the emotions, is aware of the responses, is aware of the choices, is willing to feel good with the responses within the emotions to the choices and is aware of the responses which equal the conscious alignment between you and you. You become the deliberate feeler; you feel into your imagination your desires and your dreams.

A deliberate creator chooses the alignment and deliberately brings into existence through emotions and imagination the desired path or alignment to what is wanted, a deliberate creator knows and feels the existence of the universal forces and taps into this resourceful energy to create and become more. The deliberate creator clarifies the emotions and knows what is being observed of what is, is what you will get, more of what is wanted or unwanted.

Whereas creating by default is not aware of the choices, and not aware of what the emotions is telling them, is not aware of the responses to the choices. Law of attraction then responds to the responses of those choices that are made automatically without active consideration and or viable alternative choices and options to decisions.

The default effect is the absence of the willingness of feeling a viable alternative; it is a pre-set choice that will be used if no choice is created, it becomes action oriented and most of the times these decisions do not play out to your advantage. When you come to feel the emotions within, you will feel the off-ness to the decision taken.

Whereas the deliberate creator is willing to feel good, is willing to feel the emotional responses to the feelings of the choices.

•

Law of Thought

Our destiny changes with our thoughts; we shall become what we wish to become, do what we wish to do, when our habitual thoughts correspond with our desires.

: Orison Swett Marden

The continuations of thoughts attract what you want. This is the Law of thought attraction, pure and simple as that.

How easy can this be, I have to be aware of my very own thoughts; that is the key, and that is the Holy Grail to your Inner Being and to the collective life stream of this vibrational energy, which flows vibrational energies through you and receives vibrational energies from you.

Consider the thoughts that flow in and out throughout the day, what thoughts are you gathering momentum upon, are they pure positive thoughts or have you tipped the scale to negative thoughts, thoughts are the mood patterns that dictate the day, these emotional moods dictate to who you are in this moment, they dictate and expand to outside physical human forms, they can gather momentum and create havoc, this would not occur on a high vibrating vibration. Thoughts are powerful, thoughts are vibration, thoughts are transmittable and receivable; only give out thoughts that you want to vibrate with and what you want to be the receiver of.

Think about your thoughts, how you start with a thought and then within minutes, that thought has deviated away from the first thought into thoughts of momentous proportions. Stop go back to the original thought if the flow of thought is a negative emotional thought, look at what created the thought, identify what and where these thoughts are taking you, how do you feel with the thought, do you want to go down this thought process, does it enhance you, or does it not serve you, and remember the thought is still a vibrational memory, it is to change the thought, and only think with new and better thoughts.

True alignment with your Source begins with thoughts, thoughts bring in emotional feelings, and these are the indicators to what you are feeling at any point in time. How do you feel when these thoughts are positive or negative, how does the body feel, how does the emotions feel, are you introducing a heavy dark energy feeling or a light feeling, these are the indicators how aligned you are with your Inner Being. All of these energies are vibration, what vibration are you courting.

Negative thought is a contradictory thought as your Inner Being The Source within does not see it that way, which is why you feel the off-ness of that thought, and the contrast of the thought evokes the decision, to feel a better feeling thought.

Negative emotion is the most practised emotion, it feels normal to most everyone, it is to recognise this negative emotion and clean it up.

When the thoughts and feelings are of pure and positive intent, and the emotional energy is light within, it gathers momentum of lightness and life just flows, this is the indicator you are pointing in the right direction, you feel appreciation for all things great and small, for negative and positive for you know each vibration is a vibration of experiencing for the expansion of your Source. The pure vibration looks at both aspects of the contrasting thought and the clarifying thought, and does not react to conditions, and understands the concept of each vibrating emotion; this is the freedom we all want to get to, and this is being in pure alignment. It is to identify the thought behind the thought, behind the thought, and behind the thought, you may have a thought but feel a mixed emotion to the thought behind the thought, and you will begin to feel the thoughts.

Thought is the life steam, you are here now on the leading edge of thought, the universe expands with your thoughts, the universe appreciates pure delicious new thoughts, with new thought brings in new expansion, we have expanded our thoughts to the here and now, imagine the concept where new thought can lead the universe too, and lead your Source too.

Once again you are Source energy and are an extension of this Source you are all here on the leading edge of thought, right here right now on new thought, there is nothing more leading edge than the thought you are focusing upon. This is how the universe expands with your thoughts; these are thoughts that are all accumulated into this life time reality, not just your thoughts but all thoughts, every existence of all thoughts working on the leading edge of the now. The Source is thought, new thought expands the universe, and expands you into a fuller you. These thoughts become emotions and feelings and become a vibration; this vibration is what is felt by the collective consciousness. It is to understand what you are pulsating and vibrating, you are the antenna, and this is what the universal energies feels, this is your point of attraction to the wanted and unwanted.

Law of Want

Imagination is everything. It is the preview of life's coming attractions.

: Albert Einstein

You get what you want all the time no exceptions.

The wanted and unwanted is carved out of this life experience.

Thought processes of wanted and unwanted, is pointing you to your attraction. You cannot think a thought without thinking the opposite of that thought, the thought of the wanted and unwanted is what is directing you to that thought.

It is as simple as your thoughts; you have a choice, to change the thought pattern. We all have a yin and a yang; we all have a dark and a light side, a negative a positive, an opposite to a thought, it all depends on which one you are courting. It is the duality in wants and unwanted it is what you give your attention to "Whatsoever a man soweth, that shall he also reap" Galatians 6:7

If you want more money, and have been putting out for the wanting of more money, then put out a thought of its opposite of, I haven't got the money, I don't know how to get more money, the prominent thought I don't have, and the desperation of wanting is the predominant thought. Desperation separates the desire because you are feeling the lack of money, meaning the not having of the money, which becomes the dominate thought.

I want a lover, but I don't have a lover, how can I get a lover, how, when and the not having is the dominate thought patterns.

Thoughts have the intent of the thought. Thoughts that inspire, are the meaningful thoughts, the meaningful emotional feeling thoughts, when thoughts are connected in true meaningful vibration and the laws of the universe can feel those meaningful intentions behind the thoughts and emotional feelings, the laws of the universe will bring through those wants and desires, when they know you are in complete stable vibration to that vibrational frequency.

I want more money, keep building on what I want, imagine the money I know money is coming my way, it is not up to me to know how it comes, I can feel it, it feels good, I know I have to be up to speed with my vibration, I know it is fine tuning of me with my Inner Being my Source, and my Source knows what I want.

I want my lover I can feel my lover I can imagine my lover, I can imagine that good feeling, I can sense my lover, I can imagine going places with my lover, I feel the presence of my lover, even though I can't see it or touch my lover, I can feel my lover into my presence, it is a wonderful feeling, I know my Source knows when my lover and I are ready for a greater expansion of love. I know in good time my lover will be the right lover by my side, we will be so tuned into vibration it makes me feel so gooey and delicious inside, because I know Source knows what I want, now I will let it be, to let it be is the tool, I do not have to ponder or keep on asking, for my desires, for they are already in process with infinite intelligence in the non-physical, I know they are marrying up the right person in the right time for me. I know it is all about my pureness of thought to that desire, and living and imagining the story, and most of all it is appreciating me, and others, and having fun along the way, and enjoying the presence of knowing.

My body is in dis-easement I know I can bring myself into full alignment of wellness by my very own thoughts; I now know that any dis-easement is about my very own thoughts adding to the momentum of the dis-easement. I now know it is all about disciplining my mind into the pure positive thoughts of wellness and seeing myself in pure wholeness and visualising my thoughts into wholeness. I now know, the more I see wellness the more wellness will build into my momentum of thoughts, and it is so delicious to know I can bring upon my own wellness into being. I now know all I have to do is imagine and feel my wellness into wholeness, with no thought at all to the dis-easement.

"Where is my lover, where is the money, I don't have my lover, I don't have my money, I have an incurable disease, why is it not here, where is it. OH! NO! Change the thought; change the thought". This is the classic symptom of all physical emotional persons, which is why the wanted just cannot come. You cannot put an opposite thought to that desire. Wanted or unwanted it is all about what is your dominate thought pattern, and the attention to what you don't want keeps you out of the receptive vibration, and will just perpetuate even further to receiving more.

The wants and desires that are not coming into fruition, even though you feel the readiness and the excitement is because your focus was in a dream building environment, the collapse is looking and observing the reality of the product and it not being here. This is pushing against the very thing which is wanted, that is the not having of it now, and you look and feel the lack, absence and desperation of what you want, which then spirals you even further away from your wants and desires, this is the never ending cycle, until finally you realise, it is all about appreciation and being in joy to where you are right here and now, even though you can't feel it, or see it, or touch it, just know that infinite intelligence does know what you have put into your wants and desires, and it is amassing there in vibration for you to come up to speed to those desires, these desires can only be realised by you when you are in complete attunement to that desire, this is the fine attunement of your vibration feelings and emotions, and to what your thoughts are into relation to your wants. You have to spend the vibrational currency in your imagination and imagine how it would feel; this opens the portal to the reality currency to begin to flow to you.

If you are asking for a solution or an improvement, look only to the improvement or solution; take your physical eyes and thoughts away from the problem, for the more you observe the problem, the problem becomes more, and the improvement or solution cannot come about.

What separates individuals is the tendency to give up, because it is not happening, and with this attitude it will not happen. It is the stick ability of the imagination that brings about the wanted desires.

Another separation is that the thoughts of your wants are already done, what keeps you away from the manifestation always! <u>Is the obsession of reality</u>!

Strong desire brings about strong resistance, when you know what you want; it is stopping the thoughts of the desire, and focusing on how it would feel when the desire comes about, and just focusing upon how it would feel, this will soften the strong obsession of what is not happening into a focussing of soft emotional feelings within.

Perpetuating thoughts is taking an issue that is not working out; in relationships, in blaming, in worrying, in concerning, in complaining, in keeping on thinking about a problem just keeps on perpetuating with greater thoughts and expanding into those thoughts, and really is it working out, do you feel the angst, the aggression, the dogmatic stance, the headaches, the illnesses, the aches in the body, do you think it is really working out for you? Change your thoughts into what feels good, and focus on what feels good right now, and focus upon that only. By choosing what feels good brings pleasure and moves the energy, only think for the pleasure of your thoughts not the construction of other people's thoughts. Once you reach for the pleasure in good thoughts, and by choosing the good thoughts only, will open up the receptiveness of the impulses of what is next.

Success is in the imagination and the story you tell in your thoughts. You consciously think and feel it into being of what you want, it is the energy thought form of the embryo building and growing with each thought, and then feeling the embryo build and grow from a thought form into a feeling emotion then into the gestation, this is what All the eyes and The Source feels and works toward.

All eyes (meaning non-physical) is looking through the eyes of your Inner Being, these eyes only see purity, only see good in all, no matter what they are doing or whatever the conditions, these eyes appreciate implicitly, when you are connected to your Inner Being, life feels joyful, life is good and the more good you feel, the more good will come.

Then you will come to a point where you will feel the energy of NOW, everything is NOW, when a thought pops in from days gone by, change the thought to NOW and what you want NOW, not yesterday's thought, that thought will keep you in that vibration and more so if it is a negative thought, slide the thoughts to the present and build upon what is wanted into emotional harmonizing thoughts, and why you want your desires to be manifested. Focus upon the goal post of what is wanted, and feel the present emotion of now, enjoy what is NOW, if you cannot focus on what is in the present conditions of NOW, focus your thoughts in the direction of what makes you happy, anything that keeps the uplifting feelings within.

I felt for me a shift in energy, and then my desires were coming into being when I received visions within my third eye of a house being built in very fast motion with the scaffolding and builders working like busy bees all in very fast motion, as well as my car in the garage, the universe is working on my desires now, and all it is for me to do is to be happy, believe and trust.

Law of Feelings and Emotions

The thing always happens that you really believe in; and the belief in a thing makes it happen.

: Frank Loyd Wright

How do I feel in this point in time, feelings are the indicators of where I am right now, feelings guide me when a situation is not comfortable, do I go with this uncomfortable feeling or do I step aside and change this feeling.

This is your journey, and your journey alone, you have the choice of how to feel and what feels right for you. Nobody can make you feel what you are feeling; feelings are your feelings, and their feelings are theirs. When somebody says you make me feel terrible, only they can make themselves feel terrible, you are not in control of their Inner Being guidance system of their own Source, you are in control of your Source and your Source alone. Feelings are derived always from their perspective of their Inner Being of The Self. Look at why you feel terrible, what is it that made you feel terrible, are you allowing somebody else control your behaviour of you, only you can make yourself feel terrible. Nobody can make you do or be if you don't want to. If you are tuned into the whole of who you are, nothing can come in and control or hurt you.

Negative emotion is the most practised emotion it feels normal to most everyone, it is to recognise this negative emotion and clean it up.

This is not a physiological trip; this is an emotional vibrational universe, and everything is a vibrating frequency of energy, and you feel this through your emotions.

Momentum of thought reverts to emotional feelings, these are indicators to what point of attraction that you are in vibration with, and if you have good feeling thoughts, positive joy and appreciation thoughts you are on the vibrational path that is becoming the true alignment of who you really are, and with your Inner Being your own Source.

If the momentum of thought is pointing you into a dark heavy energy, and your emotions are spiralling out of control, and you feel out of whack you are on a vibrational pattern that is not in true alignment to who you really are, or to become, the Inner Being within you knows when you are out of synch to who you are meant to be, these feelings are not from The Source, for The Source is of pure energy and is giving indicators to change your emotions, this is your mood indicator to where you are standing at every moment in time. Every time you feel your mood dive, always remember this is not The Source within, it is you that has deviated from your Inner Being your Source, The negative emotion you feel is you not taking the bounce to where your Inner Being is, it is you, still looking at what is, take the bounce - you have to keep up with you.

When you feel the off-ness to a feeling always revert your thoughts to my Inner Being does not see it that way, this makes it easier to get of that off-ness feeling when you start to think I have a negative emotion, to think about how your Inner Being sees it, really brings your feelings back into alignment.

Life experiences teaches emotions that words cannot teach, feel the emotion, feel how it feels when in a heavy feeling, feel how it feels to be in a light feeling, feel the feelings of these feelings until you can decipher what you are feeling, this is the greatest turning point to evolve a new you. Once tuned in you can feel this energy, and you can change these emotions as quick as a blink of an eye, life is not meant to be a struggle when you are up to speed with who you really are.

You are in full control of your own guidance system, you have the choice to which vibration you want, and which feels the better vibration, we all want the good feeling vibration. Vibration comes through to you via your emotions and feelings. Not through spoken words, observe silently as the universe brings through the details. When you become tuned in, and feel this vibration, and practise this vibration, and own it and become a match to it, this is the wholeness of who you are, and what you have come to experience in this life time reality of the physical, is the fine tuning of your frequency, to your feelings, emotions, and thoughts.

Be discerning of emotional energy, identify when you have been taken away from the positive emotional vibration, and positively embrace negative emotion, and appreciate what part of the contrast of this emotion that had come into play, thank Source in appreciation of this contrast, don't go back and procrastinate, this takes the attention further into the negative emotion, instead appreciate what the experience was, laugh at it, say well! That was entertaining, I certainly now understand the experience, now I will just focus right back up to my pure positive energy.

DE- active old thoughts old thoughts are just old thoughts, they no longer serve you, and will hold you where you are; you are here to create new thoughts.

Resistance to a thought: ask what's bothering you, then realise it, and work through it, release it and let it go, you will feel the resistance of the thought releasing.

If you are focusing on a problem, the problem stays. If you are asking for a solution or an improvement, look only to the improvement or solution; take your eyes and thoughts away from the problem, for the more you observe the problem the improvement or solution cannot come about.

You are Source energy becoming more, you are as man calls God, you are here becoming more, and here to expand you. You are deliberately creating and deliberately manifesting your creations,

All eyes, are looking through the eyes of your Inner Being, these eyes only see purity, only see good in all, no matter what they are doing or whatever the conditions, these eyes appreciate implicitly, when you are connected to your Inner Being, life is good and the more good you feel the more good will come.

Think and feel, until you feel and think, this is allowing the thinking to come through after the feeling. This is being truly aligned with your Inner Being.

Speak only as long as it is good.

Think only if it is good thoughts.

Think only as long as it is fun

Try as long as it is easy

See goodness in everyone

Make the best of what is

If you are struggling with thoughts or feelings take a nap, when you wake begin with new thoughts.

I love this world

I appreciate the contrast that it brings.

I feel the ease of my thoughts.

I feel the emotions within my body with those feelings.

I feel when I am in synch and when I am not.

I love knowing what I have come to identify, what I want and what I don't want.

I love knowing all that I have been through has brought me to a greater understanding of where I want to go.

I feel really satisfied and fulfilled and I feel this joy vibrating within me.

Build the momentum of emotional delicious thoughts, and feel the flow that those thoughts feel within the emotional body, non-physical your Inner Being The Source within views the world through your eyes, through your senses, through the appreciation of non-resistant pleasure in your environment, in your children, in your partner, in your animals, just viewing through your senses with pleasure is the feeling that we all want to reach, and then the universe responds to this vibration, maintain this vibration and all that you have put into your vibrational escrow will come to you.

Law of Alignment of Allowing

We are shaped by our thoughts; we become what we think. When the mind is pure, joy follows like a shadow that never leaves.

:Buddha

Now you get it! You have placed all your dreams and desires into your vibrational filing system; it is there, it is already done, now it is time for you to let it be, you do not have to ask again, and again, and again, non-physical infinite intelligence has felt your wants, it is there, right now, sitting waiting for you to come up to speed with those desires, coming up to speed with living in that desire, driving that desire, making love to that desire, feeling it into being, feeling it into your vibration, live that dream, let the imagination become the wholeness of your thoughts, feelings and emotions, and most of all holding to this desire and dream into your vibration. It can only come to you if you are up to speed with all aspects of that vibration that you desire. This is the alignment that inspires infinite intelligence non-physical to bring this dream to you. This is the abundant natural universal law it must come to you.

What holds you back from the momentum, is how allowing are you.

How willing are you to trust that this vibration exists.

What is it going to take for you to be swept up with this momentum of vibrational energies?

How willing are you to let go and trust the process and allow the good feeling in with good momentum thoughts of well-being.

How willing are you into placing thought vibration into your frequency and maintain those thought vibrations.

How willing are you to change your habit of thought.

How willing are you to feel.

How willing are you to feel your emotions.

How willing are you in being perceptive to your feelings and emotions.

How willing are you to know your own indicators of negative and positive feelings, emotions and thoughts.

How willing or what will it take for you to believe and trust.

Are you so in alignment that there is no absence of what you want to achieve.

Are you in an emotional state of bliss regardless of the things going on around you in the here and now.

Most of all how much love and appreciation you have for you, if you have no appreciation of you, then how can you appreciate any improvement in conditions.

Being happy and feeling good regardless of having the desires manifested, it is the total of just being, just being in the perfection of pure perfection, the manifestation becomes nothing, the journey to the manifestation is the exhilaration, it is being in joy and being happy, it is the gestation period of carrying a baby and the fun of carrying and then into the delivery room, it is excepting where you are in appreciation, and it is telling of the story of what is wanted, it is the deliberate feeling of emotions, it is the habit of feeling the thoughts, it is the habit of choosing good feeling thoughts. When you have achieved the art of this blissful vibration in the appreciation and love of The Self; then the universal co-operative components come together and create manifestations every minute of the day, this begins the fore telling of your story and your desires pointing you to your, see it hear it and touch it realisation of those desires.

Step 1. You have placed your desires and wants to the universe. These desires are not flippant desires they are desires that you really want to experience, they are the desires that feel so right to you and for you. These desires have been deliberately deciphered and deliberately created by you for you to experience; they feel to you as more choices, more freedom, and being more.

Step 2. You do not have to keep on asking it is already done. Let it be. To keep on asking expresses the wanted desires is not here, this is the obsession alignment.

Step 3. Now it is up to you to focus and feel this into your vibration, by feeling yourself into your dream home, by feeling yourself in the kitchen, cooking in the kitchen, doing the dishes in that kitchen, by sitting in that lounge room, by seeing your bed and lying in that bed, by taking a shower and feeling the deliciousness of this flowing through your vibration. It is all about feeling every aspect of your creation into being.

Step 4. It is all about you holding onto this thought, this feeling, and building up on this emotion of feeling until you are living that dream fully and implicitly and holding onto that vibration, becoming that vibration in its purest form, it is pretending the whole complete story into being, it is being blissful and happy with the not having, and achieving total fulfilment of bliss with who you are.

Step 5. Your vibration is living in the here right now. Here and now in appreciation and joy even though you cannot see it yet, or touch it. Always keep the imagination of your thoughts in focus, what takes you out of vibration is the NOT having of it. It is all about thoughts, clean up your thoughts. Re-create your thoughts into 'Wouldn't it be nice to drive in the car' 'Wouldn't it be nice to build my home', 'wouldn't it be nice ....' Think this thought, 'wouldn't it be nice' spasmodically throughout the day and feel how delicious it would be.

Step 6. Build up your appreciation to the here and now, to the things that have happened in your day, appreciating when you have slipped out of vibration, appreciating that you had to experience this as an experience, to make your vibration expand even stronger. Keep to thoughts I am tidying up my vibration and I understand this now, I am so appreciative that I have come to know this now.

Step 7. Remember it is all about joy and appreciation for the now, if you cannot appreciate your present conditions, how are you going to appreciate your desires when they emerge.

Step 8. Keep to vibrational persons that resonate with you, keep away from being drawn into areas or topics that will drag you out of your vibration. To gossip, or to expand bad news, or to think a negative thought, or to argue is to take you out of vibration; you can feel this in your emotions.

Step 9. Create each day, before you rise into well-being, and hold onto this well-being throughout the day. Each experience is focusing and expanding your Source energy, which is what you came forth to do when you re-emerged into this life time of being in the physical experience.

Step 10. Make a decision and line up with it, as it is already here, make it feel right. No action is required to make it happen; action will be inspired in you when the time is right. You just know, how you know, you will know, you just have feelings of eagerness to make and do; you are inspired with thoughts out of the blue. Your body feels ease and flow, aches and pains will be less severe, ideas begin to flow, you will start to create with ease, the awkward uncomfortable edge disappears, and you begin to have insight. All you have to do is follow this through, for this is the nudge by non-physical pointing you in the right direction.

The recognition of your stable vibration and filling the void with fun, not for the sake of filling a void but enjoying the void of this vibration, it is not void less at all, it is alignment, this is where it all happens, this is where infinite intelligence recognises that you are ready for the full manifestation, when you are allowing the full expectation of your vibration to be pulsating in tune with infinite intelligence and enjoying the moment.

It is a feeling that the thoughts and emotions have taken themselves outside of your physical form, it feels like a re-birth and have emerged from the womb, and are now residing in a different world, the world of the All-Knowing.

The All Knowing

"The truth is a trap: you cannot get it without it getting you; you cannot get the truth by capturing it, only by its capturing you."

: Soren Kierkegaard

True alignment is that all knowing, how you know you just know, even though you cannot see it, or touch it, you just know, it then begins the progression of trusting, believing, and bringing yourself up to speed in tuning your vibration with the Source within, which then is reflected out into the universe, for the universe to reflect back to you.

Knowing is a powerful alignment, it begins the fine attunement of tuning your frequency to that knowing of well-being.

The manifestation is ready for you, are you ready for it. Emotions are manifestations, the belief in the manifestation and to allowing the manifestation to be realised is the key.

What set's you apart from you, is when what you know does not happen. This begins the path of understanding thought patterns and how they are related to your point in time of the now. Thoughts are powerful and only give back to you what you are thinking, absolutely no exceptions, this is a very powerful energy, and the more that you build up on those thoughts and sustain the momentum the more it is relayed back to you wanted or unwanted.

Momentum can be amassing for the receptive desire, and then you have this knowing deep in your emotional feelings it is not meant to be, but through your emotions you feel totally okay, don't be despondent because infinite intelligence has amassed something greater than what you have put into vibration. It is having a thought desire of a happening and having feelings of this desire into reality, and when the reality of this desire came into play but not the way you played it in your thoughts, but it just got topped off to an even greater scenario of the same thought, that is true bliss.

Momentum of thought in all its pureness focuses even more clarity with your Inner Being, everything becomes so clear, you see the contrast to all situations, you see where the thought process is, and where it is in its focus of thought, and you are able to re-align back into alignment, you are able to ascertain the clarity before the momentum of thought takes over in either direction. You become so aligned to your desires and without any conflicting thoughts to that desire, this is true alignment.

This is powerful, you are at the forefront of exposure to thought and focus of thought, this is where you think and feel the thought, and how good it feels in those thoughts until you then feel the feeling first and then the thought comes through. This is being a conscious deliberate creator who feels, it feels the vibration of it, and then sees it, you are exposing yourselves to the manifestations of thought to the manifestations of contrast within those thoughts, this is pure energy of the universal forces flowing energy to you and through you, forever vibrating and expanding from those thoughts.

I have always felt this deep knowing within me; I experienced and tuned into my desires and wants and when I finally got it, the book 'Clarity' was revealed to me, and the beauty about this, when I started writing my energy within just expanded, and this joyousness just built up that was so fulfilling, I knew the expected desires have amassed in vibration and are here now.

I achieved bliss; this is the emotional energy, the ultimate state of being, and the sum total of me.

I achieved bliss living in my present now, and I recognised my habit of thought, I had experienced the struggle, and this was such a good thing, as I experienced precise desires, this became the larger part of me to expect positive outcomes, and I live and breathe it. I tuned in my radio dial to the frequency; I moved my frequency into wonderful feeling thoughts on how I am feeling now, on how I feel about my desires, on how my thoughts are in each moment, on how I converse with others. It is the preparing of what you are living and feeling now, and with the desires that you have put into your escrow of creation, then what you have put into the creation escrow comes over to here and you become a realiser to those creations.

Place the emotional feeling words into feeling how it would feel, harmonizing words move energy;

I feel satisfaction, I feel clarity, I feel proud, it feels good, it feels like ease, it feels sure, it feels comfortable, it feels clarifying, it feels really good, it feels clarifying, it feels the feeling I am looking for, it feeds me, it is me, it inspires me, it calls me, it is so me, I belong here, I love co-creating, I love being more, it soothes me it excites me it calls me I belong being here, I love the universe matching me with people like me, I love engaging with people, I love feeling of the momentum, I love feeling the impulses within me, I love the ideas popping in my mind, I so appreciate feeling the clarity, I love the contrasting thoughts, I love the re-aligning of thoughts, I so love the feeling and inspiring like-minded people, I feel joy, I feel happy, I feel clarity, I feel it inspiring, I feel oozing delicious momentum. I love being more. it calls me, I belong here I love being here, I love engaging with lovely people, I love the more that we all become, it inspires me, I belong here, I love being here, I love co-creating, I love the feeling of movement and momentum, I love being the centre of this momentum. I love emitting this signal it feels deliciously satisfying, it is truly scrumptious. I so love this becoming; I so love me. I love the sun, I love the warmth, I love the rain, I love this day, I love pre-paving my day, I love this feeling inside, and I love being sensitive to this energy and feeling this energy.

This is powerful momentum statements of emotional feeling harmonising words, creates the atmosphere of seeking the emotion of the emotional feeling words, it is feeling the emotion within you and how it felt, it is getting to that feeling place and you will know, because you will feel it, and this is deliciously receptive with your Inner Being and with infinite intelligence.

The words of such excitement and eagerness increases your momentum, habit of thought with confidence and a greater clarity, increases worthiness, competence, passion, elation, completeness, and is happening, and certainty, these powerful words of thought builds up the momentum, and the intent behind the thought brings about the actualization.

You are the attractor of your experience.

You are the creator of your experience.

You are here to create your creation.

Most of all you came here as a willing and eager participant of The Source representing The Source, creating new expansion of thought, and eager to remember that you are The Source (God) you are pulsating vibrating energy in a human form and you have complete Oneness to all of this. You just have to tune yourself into this stream of energy and when you recognise, and are the receiver off receiving and acknowledging the impulses you just can't hold back what you do know, it is pure excitement energy, it is your given right to this energy, go with this flow of energy.

Prepare your vibration with emotional feelings and then you will be the realiser of your desires.

Figure out what is right for you, harmonize with a passion, feel this passion into being, create the story of your own passion into your reality vibrational atmospheric escrow, be consistent in all of the laws of the universe, create a pureness of what you desire, hold onto this pattern, when you are in vibrational frequency to this passion, this frequency will build momentum, signs will occur, doors will open. This is co-creating simply at its best, and within all this pureness of intent, it becomes the natural law of attraction, and the attraction of the universal law, it must come to you.

My daughter just knew they were going to win the children's colouring competition to receive free tickets to the V8 event, and to see Frosty the racing driver who is the voice over in the car's movie. Her whole being just knew days before the competition that they were going to win, so much so that she had the phone in her hand at the time they were going to ring, this is a powerful connection to the all-knowing, this event was all in the process, she being a painter herself had painted the Frosty car and wanted it autographed by Frosty, she had been working out at which signing venue she could take the painting to be autographed, the universe had other plans and topped of the event to an even greater event for the family to be personally at the event and time allotted allowance to be with Frosty. She was not sure which child was going to win the competition, it turned out to be her four-year-old son. When you have this powerful inner knowing, you just know, this is the feeling vibration to remember, it is this feeling that takes precedence, and this is the vibration we all want to achieve and tune into.

Love
Being in Oneness

It is not the love we are seeking in another,
It is the love that we are seeking within ourselves.

: Suzanne Massee

The destination is love, it is that all encompassing emotional word that either hinders us, drives us or is fear based, it is how we react to love; one has to understand that it is not the love we are seeking in another, it is the love that we are seeking within ourselves.

We are all on this transition of finding the Oneness, the fullness of alignment of The Self that loves The Self implicitly in all its perfections and imperfections. To love the ailment in all its purity, to love the ailment is excepting the condition implicitly and in sincerity for the advancement of The Self growth. To love you, to love your beauty in all its glory, when you made the decision to come into this life time experience and you said, I will remember how beautiful I am, I will remember I chose this body, I will remember I chose my experiences, I will remember I chose this time to expand for my growth, I chose each and everyone that I have come in contact with to expand my growth, I alone created was is happening right now, and this is good because in my creation I can create anew for my experiencing expansion I am the creator, I came here to create, I came here to create my thoughts, I came here identifying the contrast of any conditions into unconditional appreciation, I came here knowing I can change the experience, I came here to create my desires, I came here to experience, I came here to experience feelings, I came here to expand me and to feel all the contrasts, but most of all I came here to know love and to know the love and joy of me, to appreciate me, to love me totally, to be in love with me, to love every fibre of my being, this is what I really came here to do, is to love me in the deepest meaningful sincerity and to remember this deep appreciation of love.

With appreciation and viewing through the eyes of your Source your Inner Being expands the emotional feelings of love and appreciation, when you appreciate yourself the love oozes out of you and expands. Appreciation becomes your friend, nothing becomes a bother, the dripping tap is your friend, the things that had irritated you are not a bother, and you view them as part of life they are the rhythm and platform for your Source to view and appreciate how wonderful and beautiful life is and can be. This is letting go of all restrictions that you have gathered along the way; it is letting go of any ailment and loving the ailment in all its glory. It is you in the fullness of who you are in every moment, and the fullness of you is in fullness with your Inner Being, it is greeting every moment in fullness of the present time, it is you completely present in all situations and conditions, it is you right at the forefront of enjoying whatever you are partaking in, either eating a good meal, talking, viewing, listening, in anything that you are doing in the present now joins you with your Inner Being, this is what you are reaching for.

Once this vibration is reached and held onto with the deepest meaningful sincerity of love appreciation and emotional feelings and beautiful thoughts, the joy that comes, and the joy that manifest in oneself is unsurmountable, it is where no words can teach, it is the vibration that you and your Source, your Inner Being knows, it is the flow of all things, it is where the wholeness of you is, it is the manifest-able vibration that we all want to achieve.

To be in alignment is to be the observer of the environment, and the people, or any conditions that is around you, without placing any hindering emotional feelings within you to what you are observing, and acknowledging it is all created, it is all right, it is all experiences, it is all expansion, and you are able to identifying and re-aligning to better feelings, and hold steady your emotions, it is finding contrasting moments and identifying the moment and releasing the moment of that thought, but is in recognising the thought and not being upset with the thought as you know how to move the thought, then you have become the master of maintaining your vibrational emotions. This is when all creation begins of your creative desires.

Find the love and appreciation of you and see the beauty in all others, even in all their contrasting issues, for they came into this life time experience with love and beauty, they are here to find their own path to it. You shine your light and like a moth they will be drawn to this light.

Inspiration
Inspired Action

By believing passionately in what which does not exist. We create it.

That which is non-existent has not been sufficiently desired

:Nikos Kazantzakis

By becoming the realiser of the emotional vibration of the laws of the Universe process, and leaving out the habit of thought by releasing resistance brings about the inspired action, this is the feeling to take that road, to go and buy the lottery, it is listening to this inner voice that keeps popping up, or this deep feeling do something without knowing why to do this. To allow the manifestation of all the desires that have been formulating in vibration to full blown manifestation, is allowing the indicators to the inspired action to take you to the place of action, without you creating the action of what you are wanting but to allow the action to be inspired within you, this is the whole of you coming together with your Inner Being to the full realisation of who you are and to who you want to be in this life time experience. You want to be inspired into action, and not dictate the action. The inspired action is the resistance to the habit of thought this allows infinite intelligence to bring about the inspired event. An inspired event is the resistance of habit of thought.

Inspiration is right there, it is always being revealed, you will realise it by not blocking it. Allow the feeling emotion in, not making it happen, but feel and find the precision in the feeling manifestation.

To release the habit of thought, create each day by meditating, walking, walking along a beach, by working in your job and turning it into a fun feeling, by doing the house work and making it fun, anything that you are doing or creating do it with joy and fun, by creating the atmosphere of being happy, this releases the resistance of the negative emotion. Being happy and with fun brings in the higher vibration, this is the emotional vibration to achieve, line up with well-being always.

The universe knows what you want and knows when it is the right timing, the timing is how you maintain the laws of the universe and being in the emotional vibration, how you maintain thoughts, how you maintain feelings, how you feel the emotions, and how allowing are you.

Most of all it is not the manifestation of material objects, it is the manifestation of this joyful, loving vibration, you can feel it pulsating through you and around you, It is a feeling of reaching an expandable vibration of elation, it is a place that words cannot express, it is a feeling beyond compare, for me it was an amazing expansion vibration that was pure love, that love was flowing through me in great volumes, then my thoughts expanded into more writing at an even greater level, it began the expansion of more thoughts on speaking and these thoughts were not there before, now I know how to deliver and be an up-lifter. I was in the stream of thoughts where I knew all my material manifestations were to be realised, even though it was not here, I just knew. This is the vibration that I want you all to achieve, it is so beautiful.

The manifesting process is the emotion first; you feel the emotion, then the thought. Thought and emotion work simultaneously. Notice the emotion then put emphasis on the thought that caused the emotion. Create a vibrational version of you and all the creative desires that you want. This is the ultimate realiser of the greater part of you that exists; this is the part of you that makes the delivery, work always on the vibrational version, not on what exists in the reality. Once you have achieved this alignment, thoughts will pop in when you think of someone to ring, it means ring them now not later, when you have a thought to do something, do it now, not later, the greater part of you is guiding you into action, act on these impulses, and when you acknowledge these impulses the Source will deliver more impulses because you are listening, or feeling it or seeing it.

Inspiration comes through with which emotional vibration you are on, if you are in anger the anger perpetuates and may be inspired to take an action that is discorded to who you really are, if you are in depression the depression perpetuates by your inspired thoughts of depression, inspiration is perpetuated in many forms of what thought you are courting, it is reaching for thoughts of fun, happiness and enjoying what is now is where the wholeness of you is, this is where your outcomes and desires is peculating, and will be released to you. Test the universe you may be very surprised how this energy stream works.

Passport

Intuitively I kept on getting an inner thought all day "Get your passport" I had wanted to change my passport back to my maiden name, but I was not financially able too. Finally, I listened to this thought and applied for the papers to be sent. A few days later they arrived, and I did say to infinite intelligence "Are you happy now it is here" perusing through the fine print I was completely gobsmacked! it said if you have two years left on your passport and you have been divorced within the year the passport can be changed free of charge, I fitted all these categories. The moral of the story listen to that inner voice that keeps on giving you the thought, and act upon it, it just may surprise you.

Health and Well-Being

The highest purpose of intellectual cultivation is to give a man a perfect knowledge and mastery of his own inner self; to render our consciousness its own light and its own mirror

: Frederich Leopold von Hardenberg

We all want to live a life of good health; we all want a life full of well-being. Did you know that this health and well-being is already in your vibration, it is into what relationship that you are in with this vibration.

This vibration is powerfully thought provoking; this vibration of thought has the potential to direct your energy to a fuller well-being and healthy life. The thoughts you hold are the gatherer of momentum, thoughts can dictate how your day will progress, if you are the thought pattern of good thoughts, and build up momentum into the direction of what you want to happen for you, or for your experience, then you have tuned into the vibration of your Source your Inner Being and the non-physical.

The gatherer of thought is a universal vibration, it is energy, all life is energy, and all life is molecules and atoms of energy. Thought is your outcome, thought is running in parallel with the negative and the positive, the yin and yang, the light and dark side, the God part and the devil part, it is where you have placed a greater emphasis of your thought, it builds up the momentum to that pattern of thought.

A belief of a thought is a thought you keep thinking, pick what you want to activate in your vibration sift through the thoughts to what feels right for you.

A thought that is an opposite, relates to a cancer patient, who is placing pure alignment of thought of health and well-being to counter the thought by thinking thoughts; I hope it goes away, I hope the treatment is working, or the medical professionals put a professional spin of portraying it is not good, this takes the positive thought and focus away from the well-being which is yours. Define your intentions of desires of well-being, and maintaining that vibrational alignment of well-being until you are in it, know it, and own it;

The Source your Inner Being within, never joins you in your discomfort or dis-easement for the discomfort and dis-easement is not the Source with in's eternal path, it is you pointing in the opposite of who you really are, that is why you feel the discomfort and allow the dis-easement of thought patterns to take hold of you, it is you not trusting the process of life. Focus upon harmonising thoughts;

I appreciate that I have come into this physical body to create my own reality.

I appreciate that I am Source energy.

I love knowing that we are all energy.

I love knowing it is all about frequency, I love knowing it is about my frequency and my focus.

I appreciate that non-physical energy is flowing in perfect harmony universally in everything and everywhere.

I love this feeling of well-being of allowing it in.

I appreciate that I am the creator of my own reality.

I appreciate that my thoughts, are creating my now moment.

I appreciate that I have my desires my dreams.

I appreciate that my desires, dreams and well-being have amassed for me in vibration to those desires.

I appreciate that I have a process of fine tuning my vibration, to match my desires of well-being.

I appreciate by aligning with Source and maintaining alignment brings me closer to my ultimate desires of well-being.

I appreciate that I am forever expanding my Source.

I appreciate that by fine tuning myself to my desires of well-being, I can do what I came forth to do in this life time reality.

I am eager to tap into my Source, and I love recognising that feeling of well-being inside of me.

I am eager to expand my expansion of my eternal energy with the expansion of my Source.

I am eager to realise my desires of well-being into reality.

I realise nothing comes to me that I am not ready for.

I know I have to be up to speed with my desires of well-being, before they can be realised.

I now know I have to feel my desires and well-being, I now know that I have to live the desires and well-being into reality, even though it is not here, in the now. I am at ease in my present now conditions, I now find ease in the realignment of my vibrational focus, I am happy to focus on appreciative thoughts; I now know these thoughts bring me right back up to speed again with who I am, and with my Inner Being.

I appreciate that my Inner Being is expanding me to my desires of well-being. I really love knowing that it is all about my focus.

I really love knowing I can begin my day in well-being, I love knowing that it is my focus that creates my day.

I really love knowing that I am able to discern my own vibration, I love the feeling, and it feels so wonderful.

I really love knowing that I can focus my thoughts. I love knowing that I can guide my thoughts and behaviour. I love knowing I can change my conditions by easing and realigning my thoughts.

I really like knowing that all is working out for me. I am at peace in my now moment, I feel happy and I feel fulfilled and eager with this feeling, I feel well-being permeating throughout my vibrational body.

Yes! I like that feeling of contentment, contentment of deep appreciation. I like knowing that I am up to speed with who I am, and yes it does feel so good.

I have come to know now and understand it is my expansion, my expansion alone, of which I have come to expand in this life time reality.

I am eager to tune in with an even greater energy, because I now know that this is what I have come forth to do, it exhilarates me to know that, I now KNOW.

I appreciate everything is energy; this energy vibrates, in me, through me, in every grain of sand, in all creatures great and small, in the very air we breathe.

This energy is ever so powerful, it feels, it knows, it vibrates beside me and through me, I like that feeling, I love that Source and non-physical work in synchronicity, I love knowing, when I am in tune and when I am not. I love the emotional vibration that works within me and when I have jumped in and out of tune, I have come to understand when I am not in tune. I have come to know that it is okay when I am out of tune, because I now know how to get right back in tune.

I have come to understand and know it is all about attunement, I have come to know that the experience of out of attunement is letting me know when I am out of tune. I have come to know attunement is bringing and even greater expansion of who I am, in relation to who I am expanding to be.

I now know it is to do with alignment, I now know with what is about me in my present time of the now, can be appreciated, even though this time reality is not ideal, or what I want, it allows the emphasis onto what I really want, and the emphasis into the art of appreciating. I have come to feel so blessed and in peace with my thoughts to what is; to what I really want. I have come to feel when I appreciate my emotional vibration just expands, and I so love that feeling. I love the exhilaration that vibrates inside of me, it is exciting, because I finally got the hang of appreciation and the alignment vibration of well-being that is all I have to do, is to let it be, and focus into the wholeness of my new me.

I am at ease with my condition right here and now, I am eager with this feeling of the momentum that is building inside of me in readiness of well-being into pure wholeness.

I feel the energy vibrating in pure bliss, in pure bliss to my very core, I feel it pulsating, I feel when I am in synch, I so love this feeling, I feel I am in the wholeness of who I have become, I feel my expansion pulsating and compounding even greater, I feel it exploding outward and expanding universally, I am eager for what is coming.

Define those intentions and desires and allow yourself into the fullness of who you really want to be, or to become, it is all about thought, emotion and feelings, and a deep appreciation of the whole of you into well-being, and most of all, it is in the use and using emotional uplifting harmonising sentences to increase momentum and the feelings within, this is how the expansion begins to evolve within, and you will feel it.

Obstacles cross your path to realign and expand the whole of you to a greater expansion, this is a joyous occasion, without you knowing the reason and why, it really is only for the greater expansion of you fine tuning your vibration. The only obstacle is you getting in the way of you. These obstacles are the indicator that The Source within never joins you in your discomfort or dis-easement for the discomfort and dis-easement is not the Source with in's eternal path, it is you pointing in the opposite of who you really are, that is why you feel the discomfort and allow the dis-easement of thought patterns to take hold of you.

You are the creator of your experience; you are the creator of your own expansion of your relationship to your Source energy and the expansion of the universe.

A dis-easement can run prevalent within families, this is creating it by talking about it, thinking about it, placing focus upon it, it is giving it more oxygen and the more oxygen you give it, the more it becomes, it is to refocus and not give it the air time, this is how you stop the momentum of any dis-easement.

In my experience I came across a dis-easement within me, I prefer not to place a label, once you place a label this then becomes a thought process, I noticed the condition was getting more prominent, and I knew I was holding onto resistant thought patterns, I knew a teacher as I am was disconnected to my own Inner Being, and I was not keeping up with who I really am, until I changed my thought process, to seeing me and feeling me in wholeness, I imagined my body in my youth and believed myself into youthfulness, and being supple. I would wake up in the morning feeling completely in no inner pain, this is me connecting to the whole of me while in sleep and in non-resistant thoughts, this is the state of pure well-being. I thought if I can wake and feel in this state then the whole process of mediating into a pure whole being youthful imagination desiring body for me really works, I then took it further into my day, and when a niggle was occurring I went into the niggle of my imagination and thought other thoughts, until the niggle pain disappears. When I feel the pain, I sort of set myself aside and feel me slide into another dimension of thought and the pain disappears, even though I still feel it, I set it aside and gave it no thought. It is ignoring what is and dreaming of what you want and holding onto that thought only.

I Want a Different Body

The mind is everything. What you think you become.

: Buddha

If I told you, that you chose this body, and that you chose you, to live in this life time reality, you would disagree emphatically. If I told you, you chose your parents and you chose the place and time to re-emerge back into the physical you would say I am barking mad.

Absolutely no exceptions you did and you were so eager to come forth and play the game of creating and remembering what you wanted to do, and to experience in this life time expansion of reality.

I want a different body, have you any idea that you wanted the body that you have, do you realise you chose this body to have and experience of placing into creation the body that you are wishing to create. Do you realise that this body was your creation to experience how to place into your vibrational escrow the new wants and desires, and to experience momentum on those dreams and desires; you created this experience to expand your Source energy.

In a past life memory you may have had an exceptional body and have taken on a new memory to expand who you are now to remember what it was like to feel this body you have now, and that the memory and thought is what is holding you here in this present condition.

The illness you have is brought about by you to remember that you can overcome the ailment, the more you focus onto a labelled name to an illness the more your thoughts cooperate with the thought, and becomes the momentum of thought, let go of the thought, let go of the dis-easement, then the dis-easement is no longer the momentum of thought, create a new momentum of thought of wellness, all things are healable it is up to you to find the clarity, the clarity of the laws of the universe, and clarity comes from pureness, and pureness is clarity.

An issue or a problem is only a problem when you make it a problem by the thoughts you are thinking. To have a solution to a problem, think only about a solution, ask in your mind for a solution, you don't have to think what the solution is or how it will come about, but only to give thoughts to the universal forces for a solution.

The parents you have were all chosen by you, no exceptions, you were eager to have these parents, you chose to clarify your expansion and have the clarity within this family structure for your own growth. It is only that you have forgotten who and why you came forth into this physical body to do or become more expansive.

Any type of bully is an individual who is disconnected from their source, it is through their own insecurity from this disconnectedness that creates the imbalance in them. When you stand apart and observe through the eyes of Source, you see the disconnectedness, but observe them with love because we all came here with the intentions of love, the more joy and love you create, you then will create a better feeling in them and for you.

Drinking and drug taking in excess is an emotional imbalance and discord in your vibration. An addiction is a desire to want to feel better. These addictions are short term feel betters and cannot be maintained. Addictions within your body create your body cells to acclimate in your body and it will find a way to adapt and will want more to this adjustment and will adapt and want more, it is the momentum process. Any addiction can subside in a process by cleaning up your thoughts and cleaning up the memory cells within the body this can take just a few days. It is trusting the process and thinking it differently.

Amplify and gravitate in or too the same conditions, and with people, you then attract and amplify the way you are feeling. This is either in the feeling good or the not feeling good momentum.

When a feeling of emptiness is prevalent within, is only a discord and a separation from your Inner Being, you cannot separate from your Inner Being, it is only you looking at a situation differently than what your Inner Being knows, reacquaint with your Inner Being, and begin the process of chilling out, go and have fun, go to sleep, play a game, do anything that takes you away from this feeling, and when you do, you will feel a different energy within you, it is all about changing the thought pattern and when the thought pattern changes you will be sending out a better signal for an even more better signal.

The clarity of thought in its pureness and holding onto that vibrational frequency and sustaining that frequency creates worlds, it creates newness, it creates joy, it creates potential of fullness of who you are, it is where all the energy is, it is full of abundance that can take the imagination to new heights, for imagination is the clear path to all wellness and into wholeness.

Education -Work – Business

It is better to conquer yourself than to win a thousand battles. Then the victory is yours. It cannot be taken from you, not by angels or by demons, heaven or hell.

: *Buddha*

This is a vibrational universe, work, income, business, education, is all vibration and in what relation you are to that outcome. It is turning your thoughts around to looking and feeling the reality of life as a vibrational pulsation of energy, it is tuning your energy into the energy wave of what you want and focusing the thoughts and feelings only on what you want. Focus upon what you want to happen in your day, focus upon feeling good, focus upon feeling happy, focus upon having fun in your day, these are the elements that bring about a more fuller day and the manifestations into a clearer view. We all want to strive for a better life.

When you came forth into creation you had all these desires and wants you wanted to experience, then bless our dear parents our family, thinking they know best and best for you, without them knowing best at all even for themselves, they mould you into their perception of life and what they know of life, and they have your best interest at heart, so you begin to live there life and their experiences and you have forgotten all that you came forth here to do, then education sets another parameter of confusion, we do need to learn how to read and write the rudiments of life, then social skills are interwoven and if you did not conform with society, society places labels on you, an illness was or is labelled upon you, confusion upon confusion, a lost attitude develops into your life and living becomes a struggle. Then the religious system takes over and declares money is the root of all evil, teaching confusion of who, or what is God, and God is the most fearful judgemental God. You don't go to church you are bad, no wonder nothing is working out for you. Doesn't this just rock your world, doesn't this sound like life just sucks, the very people that should inspire and espier your development is castrating you.

Did you know that religions perspective is to let you stand still, morphed in the old ways, which was at a different time thousands of years ago, and has been so indoctrinated and given no credence to the present times, in the right here and now. To teach a habit from the old way is easier than to believe that we can do and experience in the right now manifestations and vibrational energies, of thought, feelings, emotions, and that these emotional feelings and thought is where it is all happening.

Did you know money is not the root of all evil, money is energy, it is an obtainable energy, and it is there for you, waiting in vibration, all you have to do is just allow it into your vibrational escrow, by creating your own reality atmospheric vibrational frequency into reality, you are the co-creator of you.

Did you know that you are eternal, and re-emerge into the physical at another given point in time to experience for the expansion of your Source, and that the culmination of the older wiser part being of you, has lived many life times with this knowledge, and has the knowledge of this power house of what Source is and can do, and that is, you create your own reality. You are the extension of Source energy, and most of all you are Source, and to never lose sight of this, you are one whole part of The Source (God) not separate from it. YOU ARE IT, with infinite intelligence the masters, and all of those who have made transition into the non-physical guiding you along the way, cheering you along, with the full knowing what they didn't know in the physical, and now know how easy creating is, and creating your desires into reality.

People and countries want to build monuments of past atrocities and keep it alive, the very people you immortalise are saying a different tune, get on with life don't look back, what is to keep alive is the monument of joy and feelings, and feeling emotions and being happy, and to only focus upon the future, this is the monument that we all came here to do.

Education and religion is wasted in encouraging past experiences, instead of teaching momentum of deliberately creating and manifesting and bringing about emotions to create atmospheres of happiness. Is to evoke the feelings within, this is what should be taught. Instead education Teaches disallowance of emotions, the news is excellent in delivering misery, and then the teachers bring the miseries into the schools and create a momentum of negative thoughts into children, why would you keep that thought process alive! Wouldn't it be nice to bring happy news that evokes laughter, which evokes the emotion of joy and happiness, the education and religious system, cannot teach emotion if they are not in tune with who they are. It takes a powerful focus of emotional energy that manifests wholeness within all of us.

Wouldn't it be a powerful new way to teach this co-creating existence into education, to be taught, dream big, dream your wants and desires, to teach desires and how to manifest these desires, and to build an energy that excites and exhilarates the individual to the core, have you ever come to see something and it vibrated to your very core of wanting to do this thing, and goose bumps rippled through me and a thought of wow! I want to do this. I did when I was at a seminar and I was so captivated with the guest speaker, not the words or the person but it was, I am going to speak it just vibrated intensely back then, I did not know then, or what I was going to speak about, I just felt this emotional energy of exhilaration that I had focused into my future. Did you know that the goose bumps is a clear connection to your Inner Being, it is a confirmation you are right on track.

Growing and going through education, place thoughts of what your passion is, when you have discovered the passion build up the momentum to this passion, once again do not place a negative to that vibration or of doubt, this will throw you off the path, the first thought of your desire or dream is the first intention it exhilarated you, and then the mind starts to doubt, this is the negative energies, this is not your Source flowing in to what was so positive and so exhilarating in momentum, take yourself off this momentum, by consistently placing positive thoughts, the momentum will build and then will capitalize into a greater momentum of thought that you had no idea that it could be so momentous, always build upon, and build upon the thoughts and emotions, and feel it into the reality. The Source within loves and appreciates this momentum.

You are the creator of your own reality, you create your own reality atmospheric vibrational escrow, and this is a powerful element of energy. Tell your story into being, by pre-paving what it would feel like and live within this dream story, maintain a good feeling , and dream and create more in the imagination, through this process and the pureness of the intent, and feeling good, and feeling happy with the thoughts, loving yourself implicitly is where it all happens, more thoughts will be inspired, right place and right timing will open up avenues, you will be guided to take this road, to buy that ticket, and to take that job .

In a job, place your dreams and desires into where you want to go within this job, create it into how you want the story to be. If you are not happy within your job and are placing habit of thought to the not happy part, the momentum of the not happy will build, and nothing can come into being or change, as you are experiencing a point of attraction that is not allowing a change, change the thought, change the habit, look at the positive aspects of the job, build up positive momentum to those positive areas, this will bring about a change of thought, and through the power of the intent to the thought, will bring about the momentum of change, and always remember it is the feeling that is felt, and given to the thought behind the thought.

Whether in a job, business, education, a parent, a teenager, a child, it is all the same process, it is all about observation of what you want and what you don't want. It is what you are giving emotional thought and feelings too, it is what you are creating into your vibration, it is your point of attraction and what you are holding onto, which will bring about the process of that momentum attraction vibration.

Pre-pave what you want to create in your business, build up a momentum of a thriving business, place into thought building emotions and see it into vibration how busy you are, how the people just keep on coming through the door, or ringing on the phone, build the momentum and hold the momentum, at no point in time place a negative thought, this will just take you away from the thought building emotional creating process.

Each experience you are having, you are creating, and each experience is realigning you to you. Feel the emotion behind the experience, observe you within these feelings, don't place blame onto anyone else, these are your emotional responses to what you are asking for or observing. This applies to all aspects of life, whether in relationships, business, jobs, or a present condition.

Blockages occur for example with writers and painters, the block is only the disallowance of what is already written and painted, this is you not coming up to speed with what is already created in vibration, this is in every aspect of thought, in any process of wants. When you feel the exhilaration of a thought and you felt such excitement and goose bumps rippled through you, this is your Inner Being saying. Yes! Yes! Then your thoughts begin the separateness from you from this guided path, is you taking the exhilaration ride and then placing procrastinating thoughts into. I don't know! How! You just separated you from you and your lit path, and not trusting the process, you will get back on the path but you have decided to take the longer path. When procrastination occurs, go and do quiet time or fun things to re-align your thoughts back into alignment and then you will feel the flow of energy being reignited, this is allowing the energy to flow through.

Teach children to feel emotions, is what you as parents are here to create in them as well as yourselves, you are not here to create their direction they have their own inner guidance system helping and guiding them to who they want to become and do. Teach your children this inner guidance system; teach them to understand and feel emotions, and to identify emotions and feelings. To dream, to dream big, to quiet the mind, the still mind brings about thought, this is where all the answers are and arise from, imagine all possibilities, to love themselves, if they feel unloving, create a feeling in them with positive words, you are an ingenious creator, you are beautiful, you are so loving, you are clever, I love how you do this, I am proud of you, I imagine love and joy for you, I can feel your loving.

Create an atmosphere to love themselves even in their unwillingness to love, for this will truly open the heart and love and alignment is where it all happens, this is above all physical manifestations, this is the realiser to fulfil and manifest desires, and most of all to trust in their own guidance system and to be happy. Being happy and having fun is where it is all at, this is the vibration where it all happens.

Education is prevalent in holding onto past life experiences and keeping it alive, and so much energy is taken up with past tense historical experiences of which are not even relevant in the here and now. It appears to be the way for education to fill in a school curriculum instead of enhancing an imaginative experience. Education has become and is taking away from the very essence of who you and they are of which is imagination, discovering imagination, discovering inner motivation, discovering how to manifest desires and dreaming your desires, and expanding thought beyond thought, having fun and play. But instead we will teach about the lost lives of war, which just creates more wars, this is not expansion of any physical beings. If they only knew that to meditate, draw, sing and play brings about the flow of energy quicker and faster than slogging to death past life experiences. It is the interaction and bouncing of thought and how to feel in thought, and how to feel the emotions to the thought, this is the real education; this is where it is all at.

You bring the reality in, of which is in your imagination of what you want, in other words reality does not exist, it is the thoughts that bring about the reality. Reality only exist it you keep on perpetuating it. Reality then becomes the wanted or unwanted desires. Imagination is the only key to success.

Finding a Vibrational Partner

The destiny of man is in his own soul.

: Herodotus

Seeking a relationship, the first step is the relationship between you and you, work on you first, define who you are, find alignment with your vibration, find alignment with what you have, or are creating into your vibrational reality of what you are wanting, not of what they are wanting, but the very core of what you want and who you are, and who you want to become.

The preparation is to define who you are, and who you allow into your experience, every relationship experience is expanding who you are, and expanding to who you want to become, it is the appreciation of well-being, it is reaching for behaviours that are good for you, it is the preparation of your thoughts and feelings of who you want to vibrate with, it is having fun along the way, it is creating what the intellect of the person is, it is about the vibration of the person with their own Inner Being, it is co-creating with your alignment of fullness with someone who will share and enhance your alignment of fullness, it is creating and expanding the

lover into feeling it into being. Feel every aspect of what you want out of a partner, feel this partner as if the partner were here, even though you can't touch it or see it, your job is to grow an expansion of feeling this person into vibration, and when the non-physical can feel the vibration of your meaningful desire, the universe will match you up to a likeminded vibrational person, it is about timing and the right timing. Remember what you want and in what direction you are pointing too, is what you shall receive, in the wanted and unwanted. No exceptions.

What takes you away from a desired partner is the not having a partner, and where is the partner, and why haven't I a partner, looking for someone instead of building momentum of the desired partner. Not allowing of the universe to bring the thought building partner into reality. Not being happy without a partner, for you have to be happy with The Self-first and foremost. Not to look for someone to make you happy, it is your job to allow it to happen, and to create the partner into existence.

Tough call but that is creating at its best, and then, only the best will be delivered.

If you are in a relationship that is completely out of alignment and you are in a consistent feeling of denial or lack of Self-esteem, or just totally in the negative, turn it around and look at the good points of this partner, build up the momentum of how you felt when the love was first there, feel into being how you felt when you were in love, build up on those feelings that were once there, bask in how you felt when the attraction was first instigated, the momentum increases with the thoughts of where you are pointing your attraction too.

Any relationship that ends becomes an experience, and the fine tuning of who you are, and who you want to become, the becoming is the relationship between you and you, once this is achieved, it is the beginning of creating a new dream partner into your vibrational escrow.

The relationship partner, friends, family, co-workers that you have right now in your experience is reflecting back to you and matching your vibration, you chose these relationships to further enhance and grow who you are inside, these relationships are creating the momentum of focus which you are feeling inside, if you are feeling negative you will meet a negative person, if you are a substance abuser you will gravitate to likeminded persons, if you are happy you will gravitate to happy persons, it is into what frequency that you are taking on, it is all into what momentum of thought you are on, it is all into what clarity of expansion you are on, it is what you have wanted to experience to bring clarity to where you are right now, it is about looking at the thoughts and making contrasting thoughts, and changing the habit of thought. Changing the habit of thought and maintaining that new habit of thought and frequency will change the direction of your intentions for the better.

Love and appreciate the condition that is in your present now, all conditions are clarifying you to who you want to become. These conditions are creating the momentum to what universal law you are attracting.

To define betterment, love the situation unconditionally, and love them unconditionally, for seeing them in this vibration sees them for where they are in the now; this separates you from the condition of the now, and clarifies your intentions of expansion and for a resolution.

When you are feeling crossways or dis-easement about a condition it is because The Source does not see it or follow it, it is you going in the wrong direction, this is your mood indicator to where you are standing at every moment in time. Every time you feel your mood dive always remember this is not the Source within, it is you that has deviated from your Source, re-align yourself into better thought building emotional words. The Source always sees all physical beings with love, all physical beings came here with this love, when they have deviated from what love is, it becomes the discourse that they are having within themselves and their Source. See it thorough new eyes and then your eyes will view and observe the conditions differently.

No matter where I am, there is a good reason for me to be here. No matter what, I am and they are not in a wrong place, when you become to recognise these emotional feelings it becomes a clarifying moment, and a desire for better, and trusting this power of energy.

We are all here for the growth of The Source within and each situation is bringing you to a greater understanding of what you want in your life for your growth, this is the growth of the non-physical part of you that resides within you. You identify what you don't want, it is now to identify what you do want, and to not focus on what you don't want, for this will bring you more of what you don't want, change the thought this will change the focus of thought to the path of what you want, the more you focus on what you want, the more the wants will come to you. This is a powerful interaction of thought process. This is also the focus of believing in this powerful energy that is working within you.

I have a grandson who is happy most of the time, when he is happy he tends to disrupt everyone around him to be mischief and to come and join him in his cheeky mood, which does not go well for others, because they are not in the vicinity of where his vibration is, but if he were to play on his own and enjoying being happy and having a lot of fun, then the others would join in with him and have fun as well, you cannot buck or change someone else's current, until they buck or change their own current and want to enjoy and have the same experience. Pushing against someone else's current or mood just does not work, you be happy and then the others will join you when they are ready, the momentum to have fun is such a draw card.

Dreams
Consciousness and Infinite Intelligence

A skillful man reads his dreams for self-knowledge, yet not the details but the quality.

: Ralph Waldo Emerson

Dreams are the portal to your Source, they portray events, and they portray what you are feeling in your current point in time.

Dreams can inspire events or to take action on the event, dreams can be an instant manifestation or a prophesised event into the future to take place, or an inspired dream to believe in the event that will eventuate. It is for you to feel the quality of the dream and how you felt in the dream; these are the indicators of where your point of attraction is.

Dreams that have the nightmarish tones are portraying what is currently happening in your now and where your vibration is. These dreams can inspire better outcomes or better outcomes in thought and feelings and for better outcomes in where your point of attraction is here, in the now.

Negative emotional dreams is the indicator that you have some vibrational resistance and vibrational cleaning up to do, it is the indicator that you are holding onto resistant thoughts that are not cleaned up yet, you are holding onto the issues that are of what you don't want and the why's of an event, change the thoughts to what you want, and leave out the why's and the don't wants to what you do want.

Dreams are a powerful tool, and the indicator of your life's attraction. Dreams can be inspired before you go to sleep, ask a question or to have an answer or an outcome to a situation, all you have to do is go into a quiet place before sleep and place out to your Source for guidance, if the solution is available instant feedback is relayed. Feedback may come in the form of a dream or events soon to occur, or a symbolic thought or image will be portrayed to you in thought or feeling or as a vision, it is for you to believe in the vision or thought and more so, how you felt in that thought or vision. The answer is not only relayed by internal sensory, but by outside connections, infinite intelligence is a powerful intermediary to bring things to your attention, a series of paths will be revealed to you, it could be the radio alarm will play a song that is the answer, or a song may be persistent in your mind, it could be a number plate, a bill board, a feather, or you hear a word and it vibrates profoundly within you, this is a powerful universe and signs are relayed infinitely at all times, you just have to be the open observer, and believe.

At times a path could open for you, and you have no understanding why this was a direction that feels so off to you, this could be a clarifying experience for you to clarify into clarity to your point of attraction and how you are vibrationally up to speed with you, and how you identify and make or do better to the momentum of thought or dealing with a situation, this is the momentum of your expansion of your Source, and how in tune you are with all the laws of the universe.

Dreams can be manipulated to make the story you want to create, this manipulation is done when you wake yourself up and go into the dream and change the dream. You have free will to go with the dream and with the momentum of thoughts to the dream, or to take another discovery path, always remember it is the imagination that creates the story to your path, if the dream felt very inspiring, believe in the positive thought of the dream, it is The Source your Inner Being within is creating the momentum of thought to that desire.

Consciousness of thought patterns my own personal experience; I was waking up and placing thought of the person related to Black crows in the Evidence of joy chapter, and wondering why this focus was coming into my frequency, did I take a wrong direction, this focus was confusing, because it certainly was not what I wanted in a vibrational partner, my thoughts were of what I did not want, to re-focus my own thoughts I was listening to Abraham and Esther Hicks on YouTube that gave me my instant answer, answers do come if the thought pattern is asking why am I having focused thoughts here, the revealing message was, I was still focused on what I did not want in this person, justifying why I left this relationship instead of building up the thoughts of what I want in a vibrational partner, so I was keeping the active momentum of vibration alive by my very own thoughts of what I don't want and justifying it. Then I received a message 'Don't argue for your limitations,' it is this inner voice speaking to me. I was wasting my thoughts with the mixed thoughts of deliberating over thoughts, and limiting who I really am. This is a powerful delivery of the interrelationship between you and you and the thought patterns. Re-align, re-focus to the wants and the thought process dissipates, when there is a re-awakening of the thought, just re-focus your thoughts. Even up lifters as myself are in consistent vigilant awareness of our own thought patterns. I am a student experiencing and forever expanding me.

Harmonizing Words

The world is full of magic things, patiently waiting for our senses to grow sharper.

W.B Yeats

Harmonizing words creates the atmosphere to move energy. It is the language used that supports the vibrational integrity, and you will feel this within, this is the energy vibration you want to connect with;

I am pure positive energy; I love being here and now.

I love knowing that thoughts, create the moment, I love knowing it is the pureness of my thought, I love knowing I can say it better.

I need to get up to speed, No! I can say it better, I love being up to speed, and I am coming to understand it even more each day.

I am trying to do this, but it is not easy, No! I can say it better, I am understanding this powerful energy each day and I am finding it easier as I go along.

I love the idea that I can create my own reality, No! I can say it better, I am creating my own reality, I like the idea that I am getting better and better at it, I like the idea of being focused in the here and now, I like the idea that this environment stimulates me to new ideas, I really like knowing this environment has a lot of choices, I am coming into clarity with new ideas with my focusing, I like this environment, No! I can say it better I really love this environment; I really love the contrast this environment shows me, I really love being the teller of how I feel and what I am feeling, I am in resonation with who I am. I really love the feeling when I am not in synch with my own feelings; clarity is being shown to me more and more on how I am feeling. I love being deliberate with my words, I am eager to experience new ideas; I am getting better and better at this. I like knowing when I meet people on my same frequency, and meeting people not on my frequency, I like knowing they are mirroring me, I like knowing what is being mirrored is my point of attraction, I really love the clarity that it brings me, I really love this feeling, it brings in focus, for me to focus on me, I really like my expansion and I am excited more and more to come into clarity even more, this as good as it gets, No! I can say it better this is the best time ever, and I am loving every moment being in the here and now, I so love knowing that I create my own reality, I so love I create my own desires, I just so love creating my manifestations, I so love knowing it is the clarity of words, I so love that words are the up lifter of my emotions, I am so appreciative to know now, what I have come to know. I love knowing I am expanding my thoughts, and expanding thought with universal consciousness, I so love the vibration of this energy I am feeling within. I can feel this energy expand with what I say and think, I so love the vocabulary I am using, I love how the play on words makes me feel, they make me feel so good, so alive, I love the expansion of this feeling inside of me, I love knowing that each expansion of words is focusing me to who I want to become. I now know I can think it better, I now know if a thought is taking me away from me, to think it better, I now know if a condition does not feel good, look at the condition better, think better thoughts. Think it better, 'Yes'! Think it better that is the best intention ever, feel and think it better.

This time right now, right this minute, is the greatest time ever for your thoughts and emotions, you are at the most forefront of time, of the now. Thought is the expansion of you, and thought is the expansion of The Source. This is a powerful energy of the mind of thought, so powerful that it can change your focus in either direction of the momentum of the thought. Thought produces emotions and feelings, identify those emotions and feelings, be discerning as to how you feel. Build a momentum of positive saying it better thoughts and words, and sustain this vibration and then, and only then infinite intelligence believes you are ready to bring forth your manifested desires, it is how you are in the journey not the destination, the destination will come on how you are in the journey to the destination, this is you in the completeness of sustaining a delicious vibration which is felt by infinite intelligence. Universal forces adore and relish pure positive energy, universal forces grow and expand on the purest of thought, infinite intelligence thrive on this energy and in turn so will you.

Tune your antenna to the frequency; move your frequency into wonderful feeling thoughts; this is my co-creating thoughts of how I would feel with what I have placed into my vibrational imagination of desires;

It feels satisfying, it feels fulfilling , it feels like passion, it feels clarity, it feels proud, it feels powerful, it feels good, it feels like ease, it feels sure, it feels like comfortable, it feels clarifying, it feels good, it feels clarifying, it feeds me, it is me, it inspires me, it calls me, it is so me, I belong here, I love being, I love co-creating, I love being more, I love the value, I love the universe bringing in the right people, it soothes me it excites me it calls me I belong being here, I love the universe matching me with people like me, I love engaging with people, I love feeling of the momentum, I love feeling the impulses within me, I love the ideas popping in my mind, I so appreciate the clarity, I so love being a representative of Source, I feel joy, I feel happy, I feel oozing delicious momentum. I love being more, it calls me, I belong here, I love being here, I love co-creating. I love the feeling of movement and momentum. I love being the centre of this momentum. I love emitting this signal it feels deliciously satisfying, it is truly scrumptious. I so love this becoming; I so love me. I so love feeling happy, I so love feeling the fun in being happy, the feeling of happy feels a becoming of more happiness. This is deliciously fun; I am having fun along the trail of my expansion of being happy.

This is powerful momentum statements of emotional feeling harmonising words that is deliciously receptive with infinite intelligence. The words of such excitement and eagerness increases your momentum, and habit of thought with confidence and a greater clarity, increases worthiness, competence, passion, elation, completeness, and is happening, and certainty, these powerful words of thought builds up the momentum of feeling the emotion, and the intent behind the feeling brings about the actualization.

You are the attractor of your experience. Prepare your vibration and then you will be the realiser of your desires.

Focusing statements while facing conditions, if this condition would resolve itself right now;

I would feel really good

I would feel sure of myself

I would feel proud

I would feel invincible

I would feel creative

I would feel sure footed

I would feel energised

I would feel satisfied

I would feel powerful

I would feel ease

I would feel alignment

I would feel solid

These are powerful emotional feeling statements that inspire the feelings within to raise the vibration, say these statements and feel how you feel as you place more emphasis on the emotional words.

As you allow the focusing of thoughts to build and you gather the emotions to the feelings you can begin to focus on more specific intention words upon what you want. When you speak in words or in your thoughts speak to universe or your Inner Being as if you are at an interview and why you are the best person for the job, this is focusing the whole of you in building the momentum of the deliciousness of the job, momentum words; You have made the best decision – you have the confidence in me – I appreciate the confidence you have in me – I appreciate you have the confidence in my thoughts – the confidence in my words – the confidence in my emotions – the confidence in my communication – the confidence in me expressing and leading by my example – I appreciate the expansion in my confidence with who we are, and who I am, and it is exciting to deliberately create the environment to co-create we will draw more like minded persons, this excites me, it is me – I appreciate the confidence you have in me it is exciting we can be, and do who and what we want to become – most of all I appreciate my Inner Being and the universal understanding of expansion.

This is the focusing of thoughts that it is already done and you are at the interview, and how exciting it is at this interview, just talk to in your thoughts to your most powerful tool which is your Inner Being.

This is the same in relationships talk to the person personally, focus the thoughts with you speaking to the person personally as if this person were in front of you right now, and how delicious this person feels, smells, speaks, touches, looks, the list is endless in what you would say to them, build up the thoughts and feel the thoughts, your Inner Being feels this emotion and then your Inner Being will gather the right person in the right time to you. Yearning will not bring it to you, it is finding the balance of the emotions and feeling the momentum within you, and when you do this, and believe in the power of infinite intelligence, all that you want will come to you.

Daily Intentions

Practice yourself in little things, and thence proceed to greater.

: Epictetus

Before you begin your day, just lie in your bed and think about what you would like to happen today. It is pre-paving what you would like your day to be today, this only takes about fifteen seconds.

Today I would like to find easy parking.

Today the people I meet will be fun.

Today I would like to see lots of people coming into my business, or my shop, or where I work.

Today I would like to see lots of sales going through the cash register.

Today I want to be happy and have fun.

Today I would like to meet like-minded people.

Today I would like to add value to others, and feel the value vibrate through me.

Today while I exercise, or walk , or run, or swim I would like to feel the ease of my body, I would like to feel the flow of energy, I would like to feel the power within me, I like this feeling, this is how I want to feel today.

Today I want to taste delicious food, and enjoy and saviour each mouthful.

Today I want to feel the inspiration within to inspire a thought, to inspire the solution.

When you practice the intentions of what you want to happen in your day, these intentions will begin to play out throughout the day, it is then noticing how your day panned out, and appreciating that the intentions you imagined into being really do work. This is your daily routine, and each day just gets better and better, and many thoughts to desires will start to manifest.

Scripting Selection Intentions

What this power is I cannot say. All I know is that it exists

: Alexander Bell

Write down a list of bullet points of everything you want, and including what can be done now, and the larger things wanted, and include emotional feelings to the bullet point list, example joy, happy, laughter, appreciation and fun.

Use a highlighter and go through your list and select what you can do on the list right now. Use another coloured highlighter and go through the list again and select what you can't do now or you do not have the means to do it, these you will assign it to the universe to do, with this intention you have released it to the universe to take care off. Then look at the list at what you can do now and can be accomplished by you. You will find that the main scripting which can be accomplished by you, and you will find the main selection is what you can accomplish is living in joy, and when you find the harmony of living in joy and trusting that the greater wiser part of you is working on the part of what you have left for the universe to accomplish. The essence of this scripting is to release it to the universe and imagine and dream, and imagine, dream and then feel it into being; this is the only part you have to do, is to feel the emotion.

Scripting Creative Imagination

You cannot depend on your eyes when your imagination is out of focus.

: Mark Twain

The thoughts will intensify into a feeling of your dreams, you will begin to feel yourself within the imagination, and you are happy in the imagination even though it has not happened, when you get to this feeling this is when you know you are in synchronicity with your source your Inner Being.

To clarify this feeling emotion of the desire, if you want to live at the beach, script the feeling of the beach, tell the story of how it feels to you, feel the beach, smell the beach, feel the wind, and feel the whole environment enveloping you and oozing through you without any contrasting feelings, of which being negative feelings within you, of how, when, where, is it going to happen, this yoyo back and forward thought, takes away the very essence of how you are meant to feel, and the desire is not a match in your vibration yet. But if the desire is strong within you, you will find a way to focus your thoughts and then feel your way into your desire.

Change the scripting words to 'Wouldn't it be nice to live at the beach, wouldn't it be nice to walk in the water, wouldn't it be nice to feel the breeze'.

I found for me using the words and you fill in the blanks, 'Wouldn't it be nice living........ Wouldn't it be nice driving.......... Wouldn't it be nice financial.................. This form of words took away the feeling of obsessional thinking and feeling, and opened a clearer thought pattern.

The universe likes to hear why you would like it, I have experienced expansion and have felt and appreciated all the contrasting and clarifying thoughts, I love the idea of the value that it will bring to me and others, I love the choices, I love being more and with more there is more choices, I love being more, I love the feeling, I love the idea of mobility, I love the idea of more vitality, I feel really eager, I feel passion of what is coming to me. I eager with more choices, I feel extremely good, I love this feeling, and I love the deliciousness of this feeling.

It is the feeling emotion to obtain, and then the rest will follow.

Thrive

Never give up on what you really want to do. The person with big dreams is more powerful than one with all the facts

: Albert Einstein

To thrive is being the deliberate creator of expansion of one's vibration, and this is created by the words that are being used in thought to create a vibration within which can be felt, it is the feeling place to feel and the clarity is in the transformation of the contrast into better feeling thoughts, not to avoid the negative thoughts but to transform and emphasis new better thoughts which makes you feel good.

If I told you I wrote every detail in the book of 'Clarity' while living in conditions that were far from any description of a person that could conceive the potential of any outcome or believe in the validation of truth or even proof to come into being, you would not even consider to read or listen or believe in my story, and if it were not for the validation you still would not believe, well believe me, my story, my words, and my alignment to the laws of the universe, I created my imagination into reality, you can do as I have done through the clarity of my example. If this were all conceivable then you can do as I have done, it takes the power of your thoughts and consistently aligning the thoughts to the NOW, not rehashing the past, and only thinking the projection and anticipation of the imagination of what you want in the future and what you want for you, and focusing only on feeling the emotions to the thoughts.

The past is the past it does not serve you or me, it holds you apart from who you really are, and who you are to become, and to what can come to you. In simple words I experienced the hardship, I experienced the struggle, I experienced the not having, I experienced the loss of everything, to keep resonating with that, is not where I am at, 'Now I am here', I am not going to talk about where I was, this demonstration just holds you and me out of alignment, and from the fullness of who you are meant to be, and nothing comes forth in this vibrational alignment, it is to talk about where I am, it is to talk about what I want in my life experience, it is to dream and imagine my desires into beingness, this is the secret to success, this is where it is all at, it is as pure and simple as that.

To obtain clarity in thought and how thoughts interact with all that you do in every moment of the NOW is right NOW is where it is all at, it is the expansion of your thoughts into pure positive thoughts, it is enjoying every moment of the NOW, it is seeing every moment as an expansion of your thoughts, and the contrasting thoughts that come into play are for greater expansion of thinking it better, seeing it better, it is identifying the thoughts and the mood which you are in, it is seeing through a new set of eyes. It is tuning your thoughts and moods into appreciation and love. Universal law is all pure positive thoughts, it is seeing peoples different perspectives and views to where they are at with compassion in knowing where they are is okay, and you having no conflicting thoughts in where they are at, it is identifying that they too are on an expansion path, and they too will identify where they are going when they are ready to allow their Inner Being their Source within to captivate them.

Identify the mood, the emotions that you are manifesting into your experience. The secret is in identifying your thoughts your mood and how you feel, and where those thoughts and feelings are taking you, is this the right momentum of feelings that you are creating within you, once you identify these thoughts and can bring about a better feeling, a better emotion to those thoughts this is when you are truly in alignment to who you are wanting to become, which is to be a conscious deliberate creator and allow into your experience your wants and desires and to manifest pure positive feelings and thoughts, and how do you do this! Is through your emotions and how you feel in your mood, this is the indicators to where you are at right now.

This can be done the easy way or the hard way, that is your choice, but when you decide to allow the Source within you into your experience and you become tuned into the fullness with your Inner Being, this is when the co-operative components of the universal consciousness energies of infinite intelligence will resonate with you.

Resonate with the universal laws of the universe, and you to will 'Thrive' it is law it must come to you, enjoy the journey, see each moment as an expanding experience, build up the momentum to your desires, dream your dreams, imagine your dreams as if they are already here now, imagination is where it is all at, feel at peace while you imagine, feel the peace with where you are right now, feel the peace within, feel the joy of others who are Thriving, to feel their Thriving is to bring in Thriving, feel the joy with being all in oneness with every component of the universe, the world and all the physical beings on planet earth, that truly is relating to the oneness of the Source. This is when you know that you are resonating with the Source within, this is how you to will 'Thrive'.

I did all of this and so can you, it is a whole new experience, a whole new expansion of you, but it is not new for you already know this but have forgotten.

Ignite the memory; connect to your Inner Being your Source that resides within, and the powerful energies of infinite intelligence that surrounds you, and you too will 'Thrive' beyond measure. Trust that there is a greater power that exists, believe in it, trust it, it is not hocus pocus it is real, it is so real that you cannot put a measure onto it, the measure is in what manifests through your conscious deliberate creation, place your desires out into the ether build upon and build upon and watch the birthing of your creations. Most of all love the process and resonate with the laws of the universe and prepare your vibration and then you will be the realiser of your desires.

Thrive Momentum Phrases

By believing passionately in what which does not exist. We create it.

That which is non-existent has not been sufficiently desired.

:Nikos Kazantzakis.

The phrases used create an atmosphere of allowing the momentum feeling in, and the focus upon this language supports the vibrational integrity, it is to feel the emotion behind the words, words move energy, and through the feeling emits an emotion; it is the emotion to obtain, clarify and feel.

Up-lifting words focuses upon the positive aspects of life, these words identify the emotions within and the responsibility for what I want to live, and until then you are in immobility and binding oneself as an end into itself. This restrainment creates further helplessness. If you want to become a deliberate creator and manifest your desires and produce a better way of life and choices to life, it is to feel the emotions within, this is your underlying connection with your Inner Being, this is how your Inner Being communicates with you, learn how to feel for the emotion, and when you do you will feel if it is right emotional feeling or not.

Words of upliftment create expansion within your emotions, test the words, test the phrases, feel the feeling that you encounter with the words, feel how they resonate within you; these feelings vibrate in your total beingness. Continue rereading and rereading until you feel the feelings develop within you, develop your own phrases of positive aspects, create an appreciation of all things and all conditions, as these conditions are placed into your beingness and are for you to identify and expand to a greater knowing of what you do want.

Nothing comes to you that you have fixated upon; the fixation is a negative emotion it is not a bad thing it identifies where you are at and identifying the emotion responsible for what you want to live. The fixation is the very thing that you want is not coming to you, because the fixation is 'you don't have it,' it is being happy without the desire, to get what you desire.

The art is in recognising the emotions; the art is in tuning into the emotion and identifying and releasing or enhancing to a better feeling emotion. The art is creating your desires, and then releasing the desires to the universe for the universe to bring it about, not for you to bring it about, but for the universe to give you the indications to take the next inspired steps to that desire, it really is trusting in the process, what stops the desire is fixation – why – how – when – it is not here – where is it – this is bull shit – this is not fairy land – then where is it – get in the real world – how can I trust what I can't see – are you crazy – joy, what joy – have fun, do you see where I am…….. This could go on and on…….

This is not airy fairy, airy fairy is what it is, when you were a child, a teenager, you all had your dreams and aspirations, it was not until you reached the reality of the real world you lost your ability to dream, to imagine, to focus, and then you left your imaginative dreams behind, and the pure positive energy that was within you was forgotten, it is to go within and to remember the imaginative thoughts and dreams, this is the focus, this is using the existence of infinite intelligence to bring about the manifestations. It is remembering you are not alone, your Inner Being is with you always, and it does not leave you, it is you leaving your Inner Being.

To reconnect is as simple as using words in thought which create an emotional feeling within, identify the feelings and build up the feeling until it is magnified and so bright, this is the process of achieving your connection with YOU, and it is through this magnification that what you want will make its way to you. It is going Airy Fairy which brings about the desires; this is the non-resistant process that achieves.

Have fun in the words, have fun in building up the phrases, no matter where you are, think momentum phrases, write down positive momentum phrases, and watch how these phrases create a build-up of emotions within. When you feel a lower mood feeling within start with small phrases, and in slow focus words, build up the words, until you feel better, and vibrate with this momentum and watch what the universe will deliver. Have fun and enjoy the ride, this is what the universe feels. Your Inner Being relishes in contemplation and loves the fun and joy that you deliberately create in your vibration.

First and foremost it is to believe in something greater that exists outside of you and inside of you. The greater part of you is the eternal part of you that exists unseen and is always with you holding a steady vibration.

I am Source energy

I am an extension of Source

I am here creating on the leading edge of thought; thought is where it is all at.

I came forth into existence to be the deliberate creator, the deliberate feeler.

I came forth here for reason and value.

I came forth to remember my beingness.

I am pure positive energy.

I love being here and now.

I love knowing that thoughts create the moment.

I love knowing it is the pureness of my thought.

I love knowing I can say it better.

I need to get up to speed, 'No'! I can say it better, I love being up to speed, and I am coming to understand it even more each day.

I am trying to do this, but it is not easy, 'No'! I can say it better, I am understanding this powerful energy each day and I am finding it easier as I go along.

I love the idea that I can create my own reality, 'No'! I can say it better, I am creating my own reality, I like the idea that I am getting better and better at it, I like the idea of being focused here and now, I like the idea that this environment stimulates me to new ideas, I really like knowing this environment has a lot of choices, I am coming into clarity with new ideas with my focusing, I like this environment, 'No'! I can say it better I really love this environment; I really love the contrast this environment shows me, I really love being the teller of how I feel and what I am feeling, I am in resonation with who I am. I really love the feeling when I am not in synch with my own feelings; clarity is being shown to me more and more on how I am feeling. I love being deliberate with my words, I am eager to experience new ideas; I am getting better and better at this. I like knowing when I meet people on my same frequency, and meeting people not on my frequency, I like knowing they are mirroring me, I like knowing what is being mirrored is my point of attraction, I really love the clarity that it brings me, I really love this feeling, it brings in focus, for me to focus on me, I really like my expansion and I am excited more and more to come into clarity even more, this as good as it gets, 'No'! I can say it better 'This is the best time ever', and I am loving every moment being in the here and now, I so love knowing that I create my own reality, I so love I create my own desires, I just so love creating my manifestations, I so love knowing it is the clarity of words, I so love that the words are the up lifter of my emotions, I am so appreciative to know now, what I have come to know. I love knowing I am expanding my thoughts and expanding consciousness with thought. I so love the vibration of this energy I am feeling within. I can feel this energy expand with what I say and think, I so love the vocabulary I am using, I love how the play on words makes me feel, they make me feel so good, so alive, I love the expansion of this feeling inside of me, I love knowing that each expansion of words is focusing me to who I want to become. I now know I can think it better, I now know if a thought is taking me away from me, to think it better, I now know if a condition does not feel good, look at the condition better, think better thoughts. Think it better, 'Yes'! Think it better that is the best intention ever, feel and think it better.

'Yes'! Feel, think and do it better.

This time right now, right this minute, is the greatest time ever for your thoughts and emotions, you are at the most forefront of time, of the NOW. Thought is the expansion of you, and thought is the expansion of my Inner Being. This is a powerful energy of the mind of thought, so powerful that it can change your focus in either direction of the momentum of the thought. Thought produces emotions and feelings, identify those emotions and feelings, be discerning as to how you feel. Build a momentum of positive saying it better, thinking it better, seeing it better, and sustain this vibration and then, and only then infinite intelligence believes you are ready will bring forth your manifested desires, for you have the completeness of sustaining a delicious vibration that is felt by infinite intelligence. Universal forces adore and relish pure positive energy, universal forces grow and expand on the purest of thought, they and you thrive on this energy. Source relishes in contemplation and feels you becoming more, feels your dreams your desires, feels your allowing into beingness the greater part of you that is really you.

Now! Did that feel absolutely delicious, did you feel the ride of that energy, and did you feel the power in those words!

Isn't it more satisfying where you are going and want to become. Isn't it more satisfying to know you can create your dreams by becoming more with your Inner Being, and it is the greater part of you, it is the eternal part of you, did you know the eternal part of you is infinite, even in death it still exists, it has existed and will keep on existing into many lifetimes, this is the energy feeling emotional part of you that exists within you which you cannot see or touch, but can feel, you can feel the intuitive part of you, this is your Inner Being. To be more is to know that the energy inside of you is The Source (God). You are it in its purest form. It exists, it exists, and it exists in each and every human being. You are the powerful power house of deliberately creating your present now your creations, your dreams, and your desires, into the present now, if it is not created now it will hold in vibration for a future existence, isn't it more satisfying to live the desires into reality in the present now, isn't it more satisfying to know you can be more and bring it into existence by your very own emotions, in the thoughts you feel and how you feel it into thoughts. To ride the wave of feeling good is where it is all at.

Moods

The greater part of you is the eternal part of you which exists unseen and is always with you holding a steady vibration, it is whether you are in or out of alignment to the vibration, to know if you are in or out of vibration is all to do with how you are feeling, and the indicators is through what mood you are paying attention too. Negative emotion is holding you apart from you; it is not in relationship with your Inner Being. When you feel love and appreciation and feel good you are seeing life through the eyes of your Inner Being your Source and are in full resonation of who you really are and becoming more. Good feeling moods activate an eruption of new desires, you feel you are riding on top of the wave, you have clarity you feel so good, you feel invincible and powerful, when the mood dips and you fall of the wave your Source is still riding the wave, and is saying 'Come back here, it is nicer up here'.

Utilising the Laws of the Universe and how you are feeling is reflecting back to you what you are feeling; it is being flexible enough to move in the direction on what is calling you in the strongest way. It is a feeling of the deliciousness of the unfolding, it is a feeling of aliveness about and around you, it feels so sure and it is all cued up for you, feel and savour the delicious rhythm of letting it come to you, every manifesting thought will open to new thought, it is the thought that is obtained in the stillness, when a thought pops in allow it to pop in, and it will expand to a new thought go with the flow of the thoughts.

Every moment of thought is all to do with your mood, it is the relationship of relationships it is the relationship between you and you, talk only about the good times of your past relationships, and that being family, partners or work. The success of the flow of any future relationship is you being in alignment with you, it is you becoming more, and when a condition is out of alignment and this doesn't threaten or hinder or affect you then you are on a co-creative dance of instant shift of thought. This is true alignment this is the dance of life. Feel the signs of alignment. Feel the results before the manifestations, manifestations follow your emotional responses of fun, joy and being happy, this is the relationship of who you truly are, and this is being you on your path, this is pointing the direction of your expansion. Evidence of how you feel will come forth.

I am going to do what feels good.

I am going to do what I like to do.

I am going to vibrate so powerfully that things come to me.

I am going to feel the responses within me.

Lots of time when I have a thought, I feel goose bumps ripple up and down me; I love this powerful indicator that I am in flow.

I so love feeling the indicators within me, I feel this oozing of love, I feel this excitement inside, I feel a peace inside of me, I so love this new awareness feeling inside of me, I feel a glow, I don't understand this feeling but it sure feels good, and I like this feeling.

I know I have my dreams and I imagine my dreams; I love dreaming and building my dreams.

I know it is about me holding a steady vibration to my dreams my desires and being the conscious deliberate creator of my feelings and experiences.

I know if I am not in vibration by holding onto its absence of it coming here, is that I am not up to speed with my vibrational alignment. My dominate intent is to feel good today and every day.

I am going to feel good.

I am going to focus on feeling good.

This is my dominate intent is to feel good, and why do I like to feel good, because it just feels so much better than not to feel good.

I am feeling good.

I am feeling alive.

I like the feeling of the delicious unfolding.

I like feeling the signs of alignment.

I really love dreaming my dreams.

I love feeling the dream and living the dream.

I love the feeling of the results of the dream.

I love the emotional responses I feel.

I love utilising the laws of the universe and creating.

I so love, what is reflecting back to me.

I am happy in anticipation of being more.

I truly love being the deliberate feeler.

I truly love being the conscious deliberate creator.

All behaviours bring about responses to your vibration and well-being, even behaviours that you do not want, or even the non-approval of them, it is your choice to how much attention you are paying to them; it is for you to pay attention to your vibration. This is your singular job and once you get this and you allow others to have the life they choose, brings about powerful momentum of manifesting your desires. Each life is a vibration and each vibration is enhancing who you want to be or become.

Being more

This focus of phrases makes you feel good when you are tuning into who you want to become, and these words are also good for when your mood indicator is feeling on the downward slide of the wave. Intuitive and insight is what we all have, build upon those feelings.

I am Source energy.

I believe in law of attraction.

I believe in what I focus upon is my point of attraction and is what comes to me.

I believe I am expanding.

I want more expansion.

I want expansion to come to me.

I want freedom.

I want fun.

I want to be happy.

I want clarity.

I want my whole being to come and be in alignment with my beingness.

I want to feel more, be more, and expand more.

I love and appreciate me.

I appreciate the experiences; all these experiences have brought in more clarity.

I really love the clarifying moments.

I appreciate when I am not in vibration and when I am.

I want my reason of being here.

I want to enhance my beingness.

I am eager for being more.

I want to feel love.

I want to feel the impulses.

I want to feel happiness.

I want to feel more, be more, and expand more.

I am happy in anticipation of being more.

I am happy to talk less and feel more.

I am deliberate in what I think about.

I deliberately formulate my words before I speak.

Focus

Focus and think happy thoughts and find a reason to feel good when you wake up. Feel the frequency of love, feel the frequency of enthusiasm, feel the frequency of fun, feel these frequencies without thinking about anyone or anything, and allow the feeling to these frequencies to come through, identify how each of these frequencies feel within and then thoughts will follow through. These thoughts are created in the perfect moment of the flow, and the flow flowing through you, is the feeling of a powerful flow of thoughts.

I believe in law of attraction.

I believe you get the wanted and unwanted by my very own thoughts.

I believe in focus.

I get it when I am in focus or not.

I love when I focus I become more.

I believe in what I focus upon is my point of attraction and is what comes to me.

I believe I am expanding.

I want more focus on expansion.

I want expansion to come to me.

I love focusing on everyone else's success; there success is the greatest realiser of desires and abundance. It focuses energised abundance into my vibration.

I love focusing on energised sports people; I appreciate the focus of their focus and success.

I love the feeling of the momentum of energy.

I love how the focus of emotions feels.

I love focusing on the emotions that I feel.

I love focusing on looking and feeling joy.

I love focusing on more joy.

I appreciate my focus with my Inner Being is expansion.

My dominate thought is to focus here and now to feel good.

To feel good.

To feel wonderful.

To feel alive.

To feel happy.

To feel joyful.

To feel contentment.

To feel invincible.

To feel love.

To feel appreciation.

To feel fullness

It is to feel the intent of the focus of always feeling good, being nice to yourself so that you are in the receptive vibration of good thoughts.

Define Feelings

The moment you begin to care about how you feel is the moment you begin to define your journey deliberately. You will begin to ride the wave instead of tumbling in the cog mire of the breakers.

Define feeling words and what it feels and means to you, these words are triggers to you; they begin a feeling behaviour and a focusing point to focus on the feeling. The feeling is the first manifestation; the details will fill in once you have established the feelings of the thought with the larger part of you and your Inner Being.

Write or think each of these words and feel how you felt with each word, focus on the feeling, it is the process of becoming more in the focusing of feelings, and this is where it is all at, this is where all that you want and to become starts. Allow the flow of each word and play with each word in your mind and words will just flow and escalate into further feeling emotional words.

For example, the word Abundance feels like fullness, feels like ease, value, confidence and flow. Massage the word until you feel a feeling within. Words used will evoke a feeling, and when you discover this feeling place within you this is when you can play with more words.

Ease; it feels like flow, confidence, freedom, well-being……

Kind; it feels like appreciation, flow, worthiness, joy…..

Love; it feels like appreciation, joy, fun, happy……

Appreciation; it feels like……

Feeling good; it feels like…….

Clarity; it feels like……

Well-being; it feels like……

Happy; it feels like…….

Fun; it feels like……

Joy; it feels like……

Fantastic; it feels like……

Freedom; it feels like…..

Prosperity; it feels like……

Establish the feelings to each word, and once you have felt the feelings think of something that is the opposite, you will feel the awfulness of this opposition feeling, and you do not feel so good, you will recognise that you have deviated away from your Inner Being because the Inner Being your Source does not ride that wave. You have established the feelings and how it is felt.

Appreciation

Enjoy the journey, enjoying it in the NOW. Universe loves fun, joy and with appreciation. Create enjoyment in your life and living of life. All is love and appreciation of NOW.

Source views the world through you and expands through you. You are a representative of Source, a representative of deliberately creating and deliberately manifesting your creations, you are right here right now at the leading edge of thought

Speak only as long as it is good.

Think only if it is good thoughts.

Think only as long as it is fun

Try as long as it is easy

If you are struggling with thoughts or feelings take a nap, when you wake begin with new thoughts.

I love this world

I appreciate the contrast that it brings.

I feel the ease of my thoughts.

I feel the emotions within my body with those feelings.

I feel when I am in synch and when I am not.

I love knowing what I have come to identify, what I want and what I don't want.

I love knowing all that I have been through has brought me to a greater understanding of where I want to go and be.

I feel really satisfied and fulfilled and I feel this joy vibrating within me.

I so love knowing the laws of the universe.

I so love understanding it is all energy, it is all vibration.

I so love my understanding of focus and momentum.

I appreciate that I may get it wrong, and my Inner Being will guide me back into alignment.

I appreciate I know when I am out of tune and when I am in tune.

I appreciate that I can feel the emotional energy within,

I know when I am finely tuned or not.

I appreciate it is all up to me to focus.

I appreciate that I know it is okay when I am not finely tuned, I have come to realise that it is allowing my Source to experience the difference of this emotional energy, for my expansion growth.

Build the momentum of emotional delicious thoughts, and feel the flow that those thoughts feel within the emotional body, non-physical the Source within views the world through your eyes, through your senses, through the appreciation of non-resistant pleasure in your environment, in your children, in your partner, in your animals, just viewing though the eyes of your Inner Being with pleasure, is the feeling that we all want to reach, and then the universe responds to that vibration and gives you more. Maintain this vibration and all that you have put into your vibrational escrow will come to you.

Appreciation is an expanding highly esteemed enjoyment feeling word, it is a thought building word, it is an increase in value word, and it is a momentum building word.

Gratitude has a feeling of being grateful, being grateful where you stand, it has a feeling of overcoming, it does not have the quality of a thought building word of appreciation which is an expanding word, we are all here for expansion in feelings, emotions and thought, and to appreciate builds a momentum of emotion of appreciation feelings within. The feelings of all the emotions you feel, is expansion, and is the key to all your wants and desires.

Conditions I am facing

A condition you are facing is a condition for your expansion, there is always a reason for the condition, and once the condition is identified, you then begin to bring into thoughts of the desired outcome to what you want.

Observe and feel love and appreciation in a condition without changing the conditions. Don't allow the condition to affect you, step aside and see the condition or persons with compassion, to see them in compassion disengages you from them, or the condition. The only condition to change is your thoughts to what you want, and keep focused in what you want, you cannot change anyone else's thinking, attitudes or moods, you can only enhance your mood and your improvement to your desires.

If the condition is no longer a condition to you, as it has been identified the reason of being in this condition, and it is being purposeful within the condition, and being purposeful being there, look at the conditions when you know and understand the conditions to the condition of being purposeful. This allows the resistance to slow down and to allow what you do want to come in.

If this condition would resolve itself right now.

I would feel proud.

I would feel creative.

I would feel powerful.

I would feel sure-footed.

I would feel really good.

I would feel resolved.

I would feel energised.

I would feel satisfied.

I would feel invincible.

I would feel solid.

I would feel ease.

I would feel alignment.

When you feel negative about a condition it is because the Source does not see it or follow it. No matter where I am there is a good reason for me to be here. No matter what, I am not, and they are not in the wrong place, it is a clarifying moment. The diversity of all individuals brings about diverse contrast; it is all perfect, and you will bless all the diverse people that give you clarity. Clarity is excellence. Clarity is expansion it is what creates growth, and you choose every circumstance for more focus and greater Clarity for you, not for others but for you. Every contrast of the unwanted brings about a stronger desire for what you do want.

Solution to a problem

I am solution oriented. When I see there is a problem, I don't look at the problem only at the solution. You cannot eradicate a problem; it is in the refocusing of thought into the arena of a solution.

I feel and imagine a solution and allow the universe to bring about the solution or a solution. It is to remember to detach from what is and allow the universe to bring about the solution. The solution is already in vibration, ask and then allow being the receiver of the solution.

I would feel satisfied.

I would feel worthy.

I would feel validated by the universe.

I would feel resonation.

I would feel clear.

I would feel fuller.

I would feel accomplished.

I would feel deserving of this.

I am deserving of this.

I am accomplishing this.

I feel deserving.

I feel awareness.

I feel it is all in the right order.

Being non- resistant

Being non-resistant is to take the effort to shift your emotions to shift your thoughts to the least resistant thoughts one at a time, until you are in alignment. The universal forces acknowledge your vibration. Take the time to assemble all the components of the law of attraction and being in non-resistance, and knowing that all the components is, and is assembled and ready to be revealed. Your major dominate intent is to feel good, is to feel alive, is to feel wonderful, when you are fully engaged and are being truly who you are, this is the way you are supposed to feel and anything less than that you are off your path. It is your undivided effort your singular effort is getting into alignment and feeling wonderful and alive with ease. Soothe yourself into alignment and you too will up-lift others and the world.

I love where I am.

I am in the right place.

I am invincible.

I am powerful.

I am joyous.

I am happy.

I love this world.

I appreciate my journey.

I appreciate where I have come from and where I am.

I know I have delicious desires in my vibrational escrow.

I love filling my vibrational escrow my filling cabinet with more desires.

I love knowing that the universal vibrational escrow is a never-ending eternal vibration.

It is really exciting that I can keep filling this vibrational filing cabinet with more desires, and when I am a match to it, it will come to me. Isn't it powerful to know I can do anything!

All things are possible.

I love the adventure.

I love the feeling.

I love where I am.

I love the surprise of inspiration.

I love going to bed.

I love waking up.

I love waking up with new thoughts.

I love letting go and allowing inspiration of each day to take place.

I love the fun.

I love my body.

I love the enthusiasm and passion and eagerness for more.

I love the coming together of a manifestation of thought.

I love the elation of a thought and being excited with the momentum into a realisation.

I really love where I am.

I know everything is working out for me.

I am in the right place.

Nothing comes to me until I am ready for it.

Knowing this makes all is in the perfect place and in the perfect time.

I trust the process.

I love just knowing the knowing.

I love I can dream new desires.

I love knowing who I am.

I love the confidence of me.

I am beautiful.

I am love.

I appreciate every moment.

I love life.

I love the satisfaction with what is and eagerness for more.

I love the thought by thought to better thoughts.

Today I want to be alive and I want to be alive in my thoughts. Today I feel alive. I feel a newness of me. I am satisfied with what is and eager for more.

Abundance

Abundance comes in many forms, in material possessions, through the manifestation of thoughts, abundance of alignment, abundance of joy, abundance of happiness, abundance of feelings, abundance of emotions, abundance of the environment, abundance in seeing beauty everywhere, abundance in growth, it is infinitely endless.

Abundance in success is observing and appreciating and to love focusing on everyone else's success; there success is the greatest realiser of desires and abundance. It focuses energised abundance into my vibration. I look and observe all the things around me that I want in my creational atmosphere. I focus and imagine the abundance of these things into my beingness, until it is so personified in emotional feelings that when all the co-operative components are in alignment, these manifestations will come to me.

To look at the opposite of someone else's success will always keep you away from your own success; you cannot be a match to an outcome. Whether it is relationships, material possessions, work, education, sports, it is always to appreciate their success then it will become your success.

It is about you holding a steady vibration to your desires and being the conscious deliberate creator of your experiences.

I know if I am not in vibration is by holding onto its absence of it coming here, is that I am not up to speed with my own vibrational alignment.

The most singular abundance that anyone can obtain is alignment. Abundance to alignment is the abundance. This is where all the co-operative components of the Source Is, and where you are meant to be.

I want expansion of my Inner Being.

I want abundance of alignment.

I want abundance of being in alignment.

I want to feel the abundance of alignment.

I want to feel the abundance of fullness.

I want to extrapolate my abundance of alignment into beingness.

I want abundance of freedom and joy.

I want freedom to travel.

I want to do more fun things.

I want a secure living.

I want to be an up-lifter.

I want to observe other people's success.

I want success.

I want to be the realiser of my success.

I want to feel good.

I want to see through the eyes of Source.

I want to have fun.

I appreciate the abundance of a beautiful day unfolding.

I know when I appreciate, that the Source is in, and I am in resonation with me.

My dominate intent is to feel good every day.

My intent is to do what I want to do.

My intent is to do what makes me feel happy.

I want to do things in a joyous way.

I want to observe differently.

I know good things happen when I am feeling good.

I expect good things happening.

I know when I am truly in alignment, I can expect manifestations of thoughts.

I expect these thoughts personified.

I expect prosperity personified

I am prosperity personified with love.

I am prosperity personified with joy.

I am personified with alignment.

I am personified with abundance.

Being happy and in anticipation is flowing you and your larger part of you, your Source in the right direction that you are on the right path. This is you being in alignment, any resistant feeling is you against you. The path of least resistant thoughts is thought by thought of better thoughts. Once all the components become a match to your path and holding a steady happy feeling with ease through a buffer of time, just as giving birth there is a gestation period, the birthing of your desires becomes see it, hear it, touch it manifestations.

Whatever is happening today

Whatever is happening today my dominate intent is to feel good.

I have the ability to feel good.

I have the ability to feel fun.

I will feel fun.

I will feel clear.

I will feel light hearted.

I will feel alive.

I will feel present in this moment.

I feel everything is working out for me.

I will feel sureness.

I will feel happy.

I will feel alive.

I will feel appreciative.

I will feel joy.

I love feeling this feeling.

I feel alive.

I feel newness.

I feel a knowing.

I feel I am resonating with my Inner Being.

I love the feeling of the flow.

I love the feeling of riding on top of the wave.

I love feeling the feelings within me.

Then place emphasis on more specific words, define it.

I feel a delicious unfolding today.

I feel the food will taste really good today.

I feel the people I meet today will be fun.

I feel the energy to exercise with greater ease today.

I feel alive with energy.

I feel active.

I feel I am invincible today.

I feel today is becoming a delicious unfolding.

I feel so good.

I feel so alive.

I feel big.

This is so satisfying feeling really good.

I feel really, really good.

I am in happy anticipation of a beautiful unfolding today.

When you feel a complete blended resonation with your Inner Being and allowing your Inner Being that is the greater part of you to flow through you, and around you, and you are enjoying the flow of feeling really good, is when you can become more specific in your words. Use words that are specific to you in what is in your present now.

Allowing

Build upon your dreams of what you want, and when the thoughts compound to the passionate feeling and with such knowing and with ease of alignment, then these desires can formulate and become instantly, it all comes down to the belief of our existence as being the Source and an extension of the Source, and that the unseen entities exist, and the abundance of being in alignment in a consistent wave of appreciating who we truly are. You can build your desires in a day; it is only in a thought you keep on thinking and holding a pattern too. It is time to let go and allow what desires you have created to come together.

Effort or action creates the resistance and disallowance of the very thing you want, it is pushing against the allowing, effort is holding onto the vibration of not having the manifestation and observing what is, let go of what is and focus on your desired imagination. The universal energies know, they know! They know what you want, the trick is for you to feel good, and feel the joy within, be happy, feel the emotions until it feels normal.

Don't get entangled in others plights unless you hold a steady alignment between you and you. Concentrate on you and begin to feel the emotions, clean up any resistance to all subjects.

Alignment is the work of the mind, it is in the thoughts, it is in the feelings, it is in the emotions you feel, it is in the reaching for good thoughts, it is making peace with where you are, it is letting go of resistant thoughts, and the timing is all about alignment, and how aligned you are with you.

Alignment is being in the void of nothingness with good feelings and having fun and feeling the fun regardless of any condition. It is making, doing and being in the void that feels good, not to fill the void for something to do, but to enjoy what you are doing in the void.

I will effort and try to do less.

I am where I am.

I am where I am becoming more.

I am where I am in just being.

It is alright.

It is no big deal I will just allow it to happen.

I know Source is on my side.

I know things are lining up.

I will give up on the effort.

It is coming together.

I know I will feel impulses trusting it will come.

It is completely logical what is coming for me and to me.

I am comfortable in becoming.

Nothing needs to be done.

I like to feel the energy moving.

I feel I am accomplished into the state of receiving.

I feel the convergence of me and me into the realisation of me.

I am a powerful creator and the universe is working with me.

I am a powerful feeler.

I believe I am working in concert with my desires and with the universe.

I am resonating and enjoying the now, what is right here right now.

I am loving the process.

It is all in the right timing.

There is nothing for me to do.

I am in the state of allowing.

I am allowing pleasing thoughts to come to me.

Today I want to be alive and I want to be alive in my thoughts.

Today I feel alive.

I feel a newness of me.

I am satisfied with what is and eager for more.

I love this feeling.

I love this moment.

I love knowing everything is working out for me.

I so love the feeling within me.

I love knowing it is already done.

I am in happy anticipation of a beautiful unfolding.

I am where I am – I am where I am – to the conditions I am facing, this is not meaning except your situation, it is the feeling emotion behind the thoughts of the words of where you are, allowing the relief to the resistance that may be hindering you're allowing. It is the simple and quiet mind that allows the energy to flow.

I am where I am.

I am where I am in becoming more.

I am where I am in appreciation.

I am where I am in anticipation.

I am where I am in pure intention.

I am where I am being happy.

I am where I am in peaceful focus.

I am where I am feeling into my energy stream.

I am where I am feeling the words softer.

I am where I am flowing with the softness of the words.

I am here right now feeling the flow of energy.

I am where I am now the realiser of feeling this energy.

This newness that I feel is total appreciation.

I am where I am in appreciation.

I am where I am and I am feeling really good.

Now I know who I am and that is to feel good.

It is not about you in the physical; it is all about you in your relationship with your Inner Being which is the whole essence of why you came forth right here, right now to experience and to remember, and once you get it your life will never be the same again.

I am ready

I appreciate the momentum and deciphering is fun.

I am really looking forward to enhancing my expansion and the fun that will come and more clarifying clarities.

I understand I am being the best that I am.

I understand that there is more.

I want to merge all components into beingness.

The fun is in the journey and I feel a creative expansion of fun and clarity is coming to me and Oh! The freedom is exciting in the feeling of knowing.

I am ready.

I am ready.

I am ready.

I am at ease with my conditions right here and now, I am eager with this feeling of the momentum that is building inside of me in readiness. I know I will be inspired when the time is right for me to take action; I am at ease holding my true alignment of me.

I feel this energy vibrating in pure bliss, in pure bliss to my very core, I feel it pulsating, I feel when I am in synch, I so love this feeling, I feel I am in the whole of who I have become, I feel my expansion pulsating and compounding even greater, I feel it exploding outward and expanding universally, I am eager for what is happening.

I feel the readiness, I feel the ease about me, and I feel I am ready to reap the reward of motion forward; it is the satisfaction of being in the absence of what I want and just knowing now is the time.

I can see it, I can taste it, I am in it, and I am living in my desires. I have synchronised and tuned into my vibration to all that I want. This is pure bliss; this feels so like contentment. I have created into my imagination my dream reality, my desires that I want. I feel it with such eagerness.

I am so synchronised, and the universe feels my vibration and is giving me indications.

I am in so readiness that my dreams are now showing me the signs; I am so excited because I now know how to do it.

I am so eager that I want to shout out, how easily it can be done.

I appreciate that the life I have lived has caused me to focus into the whole of me, and who I want to be.

I know it is all about my thoughts, what I do want and what I don't want. What emphasis of thought patterns I am in. I now realise I only get what I am thinking.

I now realise and have come to know it is what words I am using, I now know words are powerful, words make powerful statements.

I now realise I can say it better; I now realise I can rephrase my words and thoughts.

I now realise this is a powerful tool. I now understand and have come to know, appreciating is a powerful expansion tool.

I have come to really understand the laws of the Universe and that thought, focus, appreciating and alignment is all I need to concentrate on, for the expansion of my Source energy.

I appreciate it is my relationship of my very own stable vibration that manifests the expected expectation.

I appreciate it is all about timing and the right timing for me.

I appreciate nothing comes to me if I am not ready for it.

I appreciate that non-physical feels my emotional energy, infinite intelligence is aware of the fine attunement of me with my expectation.

I appreciate that infinite intelligence non-physical can feel the evidence of my stable vibration, and it feels so wonderful, it is such a good feeling, it is a wholesome feeling, no words can describe, it is just so delicious. It is totally fulfilling to be so in tune with total expectation.

I appreciate I am in the right place in the right time for me, and all I have to do is stay focused in pure contentment of appreciation being happy and in joy, and to feel good, to feel wonderful, to feel alive every day. This is what shifts the energy into alignment this is what creates the momentum of movement this is what brings forth all the co-operative components of the universal forces to deliver in the perfect timing my desires.

I feel confident

I feel the rightness.

I feel the brightness.

I feel the bigness.

I feel the powerfulness.

I feel the joyousness.

I feel invincible.

I feel happy.

I feel deliciously ready.

I feel totally happy in anticipation of the perfect unfolding.

When you are feeling in true alignment and when you really know what you want and have worked the bugs out of what you are focusing your thoughts towards, this is when you can become more specific. Specify more on the imagination of the wants.

Create Un-Limitedness

To create the un-limitedness in the knowing that it is already here, is by creating a vibrational environment that it is already here, not that it is over there, but it is already in existence right here, right now.

Formulate in your thoughts the un-limited feeling, by repeating and feeling the un-limitedness of all that you have placed into your vibration. Imagine what it would feel like to have your un-limited financial abundance, or un-limited wellness, and what it would mean to you, it would give you;

Un-limited freedom

Un-limited success

Un-limited choices

Un-limited resources

Un-limited resonance

Un-limited goodness

Un-limited wellness

Un-limited possibilities

Un-limited opportunities

Un-limited satisfaction.

Un-limited power.

Now sit and feel the un-limited abundance or un-limited wellness, without thinking the thoughts but bask in the feeling of it, just allow the feeling of it all being now, feel the pleasure flowing through you.

Fertilise the un-limited feeling of feeling good. This is the un-limited feeling of being in the receptive mode of letting it come, by letting go of the reins, and allowing the path to open up, by being happy and feeling good knowing the power of your un-limitedness.

Think, Feel and Focus

Think, feel and focus in the imagination of your wants, think it, feel it, focus upon it, reaching and savouring, then reaching and savouring more, think it and feel it even more. Build upon, and build upon, on the thoughts of the imagination, feel how it feels, savour the feeling, then think it more, the more you create the imagination the more it becomes, until it is so tuned into your emotional essence that it must come to you.

Place your desire, your wants and using the phrase 'wouldn't it be nice' to start each sentence, it is not demanding but emitting a frequency of wouldn't it be nice to have and enjoy and tell the universe why it would be nice.

Wouldn't it be nice to (...................................) it feels really nice, I can feel and see in my imagination the building of my desire, I can see the (...................) and I can feel the (.....................) and I can feel the coming together of my (........................) it inspires me into greater thoughts it feels so wonderful, I love the thoughts I am feeling, I can see it, I can feel it, I can see me in it, I can feel me (living/driving) in it, I feel more thoughts and more thoughts that make me feel joyous within, it is a feeling of knowing. Universe why it would be nice, I have become more and understand contrast and clarity and I feel I am ready, all I feel and think is building and expanding into even fuller view, I feel the thoughts floating in and out throughout my day, they inspire me. My thoughts are consistent in feeling good, consistent in flowing, thinking and feeling more, expanding more, summoning more, enjoying more.

Your thoughts become so consistent that you only allow the feelings of feeling good into your experience, and how you feel this is through your emotions, once you are tuned into you, you can feel every emotion; this is the indicator to how you are in any point in time of the now. Your emotions become the powerful indicator of who and what you are, and once you understand and feel these emotions, then you have reached the place of all good things coming to you. Believe and enjoy the journey which is the answer to all of what you have wanted to experience here and in the now.

This is a powerful energy, believe it, believe it, and believe it. Make the thoughts satisfying, feel the feeling of the thoughts. Be purposefully happy in the thoughts; wouldn't it be nice to be the recipient of my desires that I have accumulated, and wouldn't it be nice to be the living example of my well-being, my worthiness, my alignment.

To reach the highest state of beingness is to have lessor resistant thoughts, all thoughts are positive, look at others in positive thoughts for they are where they are, observe the world in positive-ness, everything is where it is, major events are just the balancing of the planet, even though it is hard to consider that the plights of others is exactly where they chose to be, to experience for their own expansion of growth, all is as it is, all is chosen for their point of attracting for their own expansion. Once this understanding is fully understood, this is when you have become fully aligned with your Source, this is when you can be and do whatever your desires are calling you too. Everything in life is a choice, the choice is to take this route or to take the other route, and the choice is in how you feel within when you do it, does it put you on a higher vibration, or does it not, you are the chooser of the circumstances, you are the chooser of the contrast to gain greater clarity.

A very good analogy is the algebra ruler, you stand at the point of zero in the centre of the ruler one end is the negative the other being the positive, place yourself in the middle, you have the choice of looking towards the negative thought or to turn around and look at the positive thought, you have the choice to which direction you want to go, think and feel to the positive end of the ruler and to keep focused on the steps in this direction is where it all happens. The more you look at the negative end the more you want to build upon the positive end. It is all about learning emotions, this is the emotions that you feel on all subjects.

A good example is when you think about God you either dance with joy, or tighten up inside, the tightening feeling inside is you being in resistance to who God is, and God certainly does not reside on a throne, for you are God, you are it. You are fighting against the very thing that you're God Source your Inner Being knows who you are. When you feel your heart and body is lighter it is you and your Inner Being in agreeance with the thought.

Test your feelings, test how an action and the re-action to the thought, and how it feels within, did it feel good or did it feel terrible, once you become sensitive to feeling the feelings and how it felt, is being truly the deliberate creator of your experiences, and this is to feel the feelings in the manifestations of all the emotions you feel.

Being a Conscious Deliberate Creator or Being the Default Creator

A conscious deliberate creator is aware of the emotions, is aware of the responses, is aware of the choices, is willing to feel good with the responses within the emotions to the choices and is aware of the responses which equal the conscious alignment between you and you. You become the deliberate feeler and you choose what feels good, and you can feel what motion is viable and you recognise it.

A deliberate creator chooses the alignment and deliberately brings into existence through emotions and imagination the desired path or alignment to what is wanted, a deliberate creator knows and feels the existence of the universal forces and taps into this resourceful energy to create and become more. The deliberate creator clarifies the emotions and knows what is being observed of what is, is what you will get more of what is wanted or unwanted.

Whereas creating by default is not aware of the choices, and not aware of what the emotions is telling them, is not aware of the responses to the choices. Law of attraction then responds to the responses of those choices that are made automatically without active consideration and or viable alternative choices and options.

The default effect is the absence of the willingness of feeling a viable alternative; it is a pre-set choice that will be used if no choice is created.

Whereas the deliberate creator is willing to feel good, is willing to feel the emotional responses to the feelings of the choices.

What holds back a deliberate creator apart from obtaining the desired manifestations is the observing of the not having of it, and or trying to make it happen. It is to what emotion you are courting and is the indicator of where you are at. When you do not have what you want it is the practised emotion of what you are focusing upon, the wanted and unwanted.

The trick is to change the phrases and build upon and build upon the good feeling thoughts, until your feelings are so in alignment that the universe will provide the improvement, what holds you away is then you observe what is, and it then becomes what is.

You summon everyone and everything to you because it is a practised vibration you draw them to you for expansion to focus onto what you really want, all of the summoning has helped you to clarify what you prefer, and the trick is to focus on what you would prefer.

What happens is that you keep focus on what you don't like or the dislike of someone or of a condition this just keeps the momentum of thought of more of the same; the trick is to change the thought to what you really want.

When you are unhappy the more unhappy comes to you, if you are happy, more happy comes to you. All these emotions you summon them, because it is your practised vibration you draw them to you for expansion for you to focus onto what you really want. Improvement does not come from others improvement. It only comes from you improving your alignment you solicit everything into your experience, for your clarity solicits manifestations of emotions which in turn brings about the manifestation of the things you want.

Say you observe a person you don't like how he/she treats me, I don't like this ..... I don't like that....

The trick is to reword your thoughts to; I really want to be treated well, I want joy and fun, I want to have joy, I want to feel the deliciousness inside of me, I want to feel happiness when we are together....

When observing a person who is un-well and unhappy, and they are in the vibration of negativity, see them with compassion for seeing with compassion is seeing through the eyes of Source in knowing where they are going and not where they are. Compassion is seeing through the eyes of Source is alignment without losing your own alignment.

I don't like where I live....to.....

I know my living conditions will improve; I want to have a place of freedom, a place to do and be what I want to be, a home that feels really nice and welcome.

I have a headache, my head hurts......to......I feel the ease flowing through my head, I feel a glow permeating around me, I feel a freedom of floating, I feel bright, I feel a gentle wellness around me, I feel the energy vibrating within me, I feel so good……

When asked to go somewhere, and you are overcome with a feeling of not wanting to go…Trust the feeling your inner self is guiding you… if you feel happy and joyful…your Inner Being is in alignment of the choice.

Trust and learn to be guided into how you are feeling or want to feel, if it feels right go with that feeling, if it feels awful trust your instincts.

Most of all is to feel good, it is to feel good, and it is to feel good, it is to say it better, to do it better, to have fun, and to celebrate all the emotions before the desired manifestation comes. It is the joy in the journey.

The manifesting process is the emotion first; you feel the emotion, then the thought. Thought and emotion work simultaneously. Notice the emotion then put emphasis on the thought that caused the emotion. Create a vibrational version of you and all the creative desires that you want, This is the ultimate residence of the greater part of you that exists this is the part of you that makes the delivery, work always on the vibrational version, not on what exists in the reality. Once you have achieved this alignment, thoughts will pop in when you think of someone to ring, it means ring them now not later, when you have a thought to do something, do it now, not later, the greater part of you is guiding you into action, act on these impulses, and when you acknowledge these impulses the Source will deliver more impulses because you are listening, or feeling it or seeing it. Acclimate to the vibration, acclimate and adjust to the new change. You are never alone.

You are being watched

Sounds kind of nutty, spooky or off the planet that these non-seen entities are watching us, it is collective consciousness of energy feeling the vibration of what we are emitting. They feel the vibration and they expand with our thoughts, thoughts is energy they love the deliciousness of a new thought, they love to see the formulation coming together in our thoughts, and they take immense joy when we are riding the wave of positive momentum. They feel the desirability and joy of seeing through our viewing eyes and The Source feels the pleasure we feel. When we expand, they expand, when we are truly in alignment of feeling really, really good, the universal forces will move vast energies in our direction so we may fulfil our desires.

Acknowledge that the universal forces are feeling and watching us.

I appreciate they are there with me assisting me.

Inspiring me.

Guiding me.

Having fun with me.

Aware of me.

Loving me.

Uplifting me.

Having fun with me.

Loving me.

Guiding me.

Aware of me.

Inspiring me.

Loving me.

Watching me.

Knowing me.

Knows my worthiness.

Knows my wellness.

Knows my goodness.

Laughing with me.

Loving with me.

Creating with me.

Seeing with me.

Feeling with me.

Enjoying with me.

Assisting me.

Expanding with me.

Appreciating with me.

Basking with me.

Eager to experience with me.

Create an endless loop of acknowledgement and appreciation of harmonising phrases. These phrases are felt and acknowledged by all the co-operative components of the universal forces.

Suzanne's Thriving Phrases

I achieved bliss living in my present now, and I recognised my habit of thought, I had experienced the struggle, and this was such a good thing, as I experienced precise desires, this became the larger part of me to expect positive outcomes, and I live and breathe it. I tuned in my radio dial to the frequency; I moved my frequency into wonderful feeling thoughts. I focused only on the feeling emotions of the vibration not on any desire or condition but the feeling of being on the centre stage of all that I had created in my vibration, and pulsating and magnifying this emotion of energy outwards, most of all basking in it;

It feels so satisfying and fulfilling right now, I feel the clarity within, I am so proud, it feels good, it feels like ease, it feels sure, it feels comfortable, it feels natural, it feels effortless, it feels steady, it is clarifying, it feels really good, it feels clarifying, it feeds me, it is me, it inspires me, it calls me, it is so me, I belong here, I love being, I love co-creating, I love being more, I love this feeling, it soothes me it excites me it calls me, I belong being here, I love feeling of the momentum, I love feeling the impulses within me, I love the ideas popping in my mind, I love the subliminal thoughts they inspire me, I appreciate the feelings I feel, I love knowing when I feel out of balance, I love knowing when I am in balance, I love feeling the contrasting feelings, I so appreciate the clarity, I love bringing myself back into alignment, I so love being a representative of Source, I so love the interaction between me and me, I so love the joy that I feel with my thoughts, I so love the clarity, it inspires this feeling within me, isn't this simply oozing delicious momentum. I love being more, it inspires me, it calls me, I belong here, I love being here, I love engaging with my Source, I love the more that I become the more comes, it is un-limited, it is un-limited choices, it is un-limited resources, it represents me, it inspires me, I belong here, I love being here, I love co-creating, I love the feeling of movement and momentum, I love being the centre of this momentum. I love emitting this signal it feels deliciously satisfying, it is truly scrumptious. I so love this becoming, I so love me. I love knowing I am in Oneness with my Source. I love being me in complete consciousness of my Inner Being, I love being The Source (God) I love resonating pure thoughts. I am special, I am wholeness.

This is powerful momentum statements of emotional feeling harmonising words that is deliciously receptive with infinite intelligence, the desires the conditions were all left out of the equation only the emotional feeling was emitted, your desires are already known, this is the allowing process, of building up the emotional feelings of emotion in an endless loop of phrases which creates momentum of energy, then soften the words and feel the softness of love and appreciation within all phrases, bask within the feelings, enjoy the feelings. Then STOP, BACK OFF, do whatever is required for you to do with your daily commitments, with good feelings, and when the impulse comes with the good feeling thoughts about what you are creating as your desire, build up the momentum again and bring yourself to an even greater expansion and then STOP, BACK OFF, let it go and let the universe bring the desires together, all you have to do is replay again and again until you have such clarity of the manifested feelings and immensely satisfied within all your thoughts and feelings into alignment, and maintain this alignment, practise it and know it.

You can ask your Inner Being I would like to know what is next for my (abundance/job/car/etc …) and then leave it alone and feel the emotions.

The words of such excitement and eagerness increases your momentum, habit of thought with confidence and a greater clarity, increases worthiness, competence, passion, elation, completeness, and is happening, and certainty, these powerful words of thought builds up the momentum, and the intent behind the thought brings about the actualization. Find your own effective process of positive phrases, it is all about what makes you feel good.

You are the attractor of your experience.

You are the creator and author of your experience.

You are here to create your creation and imagine them into beingness.

You are here to remember this powerful vibration of energy.

You are here to know your inner guidance system of feelings.

You are here to be the conscious deliberate creator, and to create your story into beingness, and to trust the process, and most of all is to STOP and BACK OFF and allow the universe to flow it to you. Your single job only is to dream and vibrate it into being, and to feel good in the process.

Imagination

When you know what you want, and the intent behind what you really want, it is then the process of thinking, feeling and imagining it into beingness, think and feel the whole desired imagination with such enthusiasm of just the idea of it into a vibrational reality, I am not kidding it is dreaming the imagined desire into such a vibrational reality, that you can feel it, you can see it, you can smell it, you can see and feel the colours, it is bringing the picture of what you want into such detail on a vibrational level that you are living in it, and driving in it, and feeling so happy in the not having, and you have gathered such a vibrational imagination of the desire that it feels so normal and so real, and you are living and doing it, being it and feeling the whole essences of the imagination into such detail, and feeling so happy with the imagination and feeling it is already here. This feeling is shifting the energy into an expanded vibration, and you can feel it, it is all about you learning to feel, and to feel the emotions.

This is how you create the momentum of the non-physical vibration to activate the desires into the physical reality.

Dream your car, into the imagination, drive your car, feel the rubber on the road, feel the power of the motor, smell the leather, sit in the seat feel how it moulds around you, feel your foot on the pedal, feel the flow of the power of the car.

Dream your home, build the foundation, feel the warmth, see the colours, feel the view from all the windows, feel and drive the car into the garage, see yourself in the kitchen, feel the bedroom, have a shower in the bathroom, live and feel the house into complete realness in the vibrational imagination.

Dream your lover; build a picture of the person you want into such detail, you know what you don't want in a lover through the process of the relationships you have had, now it is building a lover in your imagination into such detail of the relationship you want, and imagine only what you want, build upon on only what you want, it is not to bring up what you don't want, this will only bring you the same, your thoughts and the intent behind the thoughts is to focus only upon what you desire in a relationship.

This process is the process of being the deliberate creator, deliberately creating the imagination of the desires into the reality, this is the greater part of you who exists within you the non-physical part of you who is guiding you always, is living in the desire already and enjoying every detail of your creation, and is waiting for you to come into complete alignment with your own thoughts, imagination, feeling and emotions, and the intent behind the thoughts, until your thought process is so aligned, you will then be the realiser of your desires. If you are not aligned with your imagined desires it will stay in vibration and come into existence when you re-emerge into another life time, wouldn't it be really nice to live it in this lifetime.

I dreamed and imagined all my desires into such detail, even when the desires were not quite aligned, I knew it and I felt it, I just knew I had more fine tuning of my desires. It took a process of sifting through and sorting out and when I sifted and sorted, my imagination started to grow, and thoughts started guiding me to expand my thoughts to look here, observe this, imagine more, I then felt this inner happiness building within, even though it wasn't here I just knew it was coming, my desires were big and I knew every component of them had to come into alignment. I thought thoughts of some homes, but nothing was really aligning in the thoughts to expand the desire, until I happened to see a section, then the expansion was immense, I was designing and expanding on the design until my imagined thought was so aligned and feeling the deliciousness of the home, and incredibly excited and happy with every detail, even though the conditions hadn't changed, my perception into feeling happy and joyful did. I felt more was needed for me to come into more alignment on my vocation of speaking and being an up-lifter, which I was leaving to evolve for later, until I had visions of me speaking coming into fuller view, and when I started to expand into this feeling, more came and even more, and I began to feel and know how I was to speak. I reached the point of smiling and being happy with the knowing that I had reached alignment and maintained the alignment.

I always knew of the un-limited financial abundance that was coming to me, I just had to allow myself to get into alignment with this desire, and the compilation of all the desires were all part of the greater picture of me, but above all else, it was all the experiences I had experienced of me coming into alignment and how I did it, and now I understand it, it is now very easy, just think and feel and imagine and be happy, and recognising the momentum, for me to be the teacher the up-lifter and the deliberate creator of me I experienced it all.

Imagination is the key to all things, I imagined, and I received. I was inspired and wrote two books while living without the desires and all within conditions that could have kept me where I was. I believed my dream and built upon the aliveness into the imagination, I felt good without the change of the conditions, I rose above the conditions I was observing and kept as best away from the observational conditions, when the conditions were intrusive, I swam, I biked, I walked, I imagined, I dreamed, I thought upon the essence of why I wanted it, what it would feel like to have those desires, to feel every detail into focus and see it building in my mind, seeing the joy it is bringing to others. I listened to Abraham non-physical coming through Esther Hicks, I studied the laws of the universe, I lived by the laws, and why? Because I always knew and I always knew the vibration and the responses I was vibrating from a young age, I was just deflected away from what I already knew of the vibration of the non-physical with the reality of life.

Take the leap of faith and you too will ride the wave, and always remember you are eternal, and will re-emerge into the physical at another given point in time to experience for the expansion of your Source, and that the culmination of the older wiser part being of you, has lived many life times with this knowledge, and has the knowledge of this power house of what Source is and can do, and that you can tap into this power house. You are the extension of Source energy, and most of all you are Source, and to never lose sight of this, you are one whole part of The Source (God) not separate from it. YOU ARE IT, with infinite intelligence the masters, and all of those who have made transition into the non-physical guiding you along the way, cheering you along, with the full knowing what they didn't know in the physical, and now know how easy creating is, and creating your desires into reality.

I receive one liner words out of the blue, and when I receive them they are words I have not heard of before, I received the word 'Interment' and wrote it down when it came to me in bed, as I knew it was a message. The dictionary says it is 'the burial of a corpse in a grave or tomb, typically with funeral rites' I knew explicitly the old me was gone and I had expanded into an even greater expansion, and I felt the momentum of this within me.

I do receive many messages of thought, and I certainly love this quote;

'You are bringing the reality in, of which is in your imagination of what you want, in other words reality does not exist, it is the thoughts that bring about the reality. Reality only exists if you keep on perpetuating it. Reality then becomes the wanted or unwanted desires.'

Riding the Wave

Wouldn't it be nice to ride on the wave, wouldn't it be nice to ride over the breakers, and to not fall and be tumbled into the cog mire of others reality, and opinions, wouldn't it be nice to dip into the cog mire to know that another wave is coming and that you can ride the wave again, and that each dip is clarifying another contrasting moment of the good feeling thoughts and the not so good feeling thoughts. Wouldn't it be nice to ride the wave longer and then to stretch the wave even further. This is the momentum of the vibrational frequency and to what frequency emotional vibration that you are riding; you have the choice to take the ride or to reside in the breakers being in the tumble-ness, which feeling feels good, being tumbled or on top of the wave riding it in all its glory. This is the analogy that best represents what the emotions of where your thoughts are at.

You are where you are, in the stillness of the ocean, deciphering all that you want, and feeling into being the desires and creating the wave until such stage you are riding the wave, once you are riding the wave it is the feeling of thought and thoughts that either drops you into the breakers or you ride over the breakers with little effect, it is okay to dip into the breakers for these are clarifying moments, and each clarifying moment is more clarifying moments to who you want to become. This is how the frequency of emotions and thoughts feel, once you are truly aligned into feeling all these emotions you know when you have dipped to a lower frequency, it feels decidedly awful, you feel the awfulness resonating through you, this is how you know when you are tuned in or not. It is deciphering what created the momentum of this feeling, this feeling is the feeling that you have slipped into the breakers and that the larger part of you the Source has not joined you in that thought or feeling, it is you who has strayed out of frequency, the frequency of feeling good is where it is all at, and when you have slipped of the wave, it is feeling your way back into feeling good, or re-focusing the thoughts that hindered the feeling.

Most persons are riding in the cog-mire and are being tumbled even further into the breakers without even knowing how to feel, all that is felt is the momentum of their thoughts and everyone else's thoughts and opinions. But truly when you get the handle of really – really – really feeling emotions and the frequency to every emotion and thought you will seldom fall into the breakers, before this happens you will feel the momentum of this feeling and you will catch it in the early stages, and you will clarify how this feeling came into beingness and you will re-focus the thought, and if the thought is gaining greater momentum, meditate, take a walk, go to sleep, or say harmonising words to pivot the thought back into better feelings.

Feelings are not tangible, it is the manifestation of emotion, and vibration is a thought that manifests an emotion. This in turn creates action. It is to take pleasure in the thought or thoughts. It is to feel good in clarity.

It is to feel good in feelings.

It is to feel good in appreciation.

It is to feel good in just being.

It is to feel good to feel good.

Feeling good is self-empowerment.

It is a feeling experience.

Feeling good is freedom. Once you attain this feeling good to feel good with appreciation, within a short time life will change and the desires that you are asking for will become.

The trick is to feel good now!

This is not a trick; the trick is not to keep you where you are, but to allow the appreciation of who you truly are to be felt by all the co-operative components of the universe to deliver in perfect timing your alignment into your beingness with what you have asked for.

I will re-iterate the process again; emotion first – followed by the feelings – then the thought – and the imagination the dream, is the vibration and is the most powerful tool that you will ever need, it is the whole of you, it is you, you just have to find it and feel it, and once you do you have the powerfulness within to deliberately create your life and what you want into beingness and the key is in the imagination.

Imagination is the only success

You are bringing the reality in, of which is in your imagination of what you want, in other words reality does not exist, it is the thoughts that bring about the reality. Reality only exists if you keep on perpetuating it. Reality then becomes the wanted or unwanted desires.

: Suzanne Massee

The true sign of intelligence is not knowledge but imagination

: Albert Einstein

By believing passionately in what which does not exist. We create it.

That which is non-existent has not been sufficiently desired

:Nikos Kazantzakis

Abraham

My deepest appreciation that created and took my expansion to new heights was the teachings by Abraham, infinite intelligence in the non-physical working through Esther Hicks in the physical. Nothing is more pleasing than to listen to Abraham and to tune into an even higher vibrational energy.

It is the supreme art of the teacher to awaken joy in creative expression and knowledge.

: Albert Einstein

Suzanne's synopsis

It is a repetition of speaking, and repetitive words in writing, it is through repetition that some form of recognition will finally attune you into your Source, your Inner Being, re-read and re-read the connection will, and does happen it is all up to you and you alone.

More Inspiring Books by the Author

'Thoughts Create'

978-0-6483675-5-0 paperback

978-0-6483675-4-3 eBook

This is who you really are;

You are a vortex of energy residing in a physical house to expand your consciousness which is eternal.

You were eager to play the dance and to remember your vortex of energy.

This vortex of energy knows what you desire and when you want to leave this physical house and how.

You knew you could tap into this stream of energy and create with your thoughts and emotions to communicate with your vortex, you knew you could imagine whatever you wanted to be and do, and you knew you could trust the process and your vortex of energy will orchestrate the event.

You are the beholder of your thoughts.

Look at your thoughts, and you will discover everything that you are living is created by you, and not by anyone else.

These powerful thoughts are created by you, and to every thought there is an opposite, and with every thought is followed by an emotion.

Makes you kind of want to think about what you are thinking about.

'Amplifying Thoughts'

978-0-6483420-2-1 eBook

978-0-6483420-7-6 paperback

Everything is thought. You will discover your mind is thought and every thought is creation, your thoughts can be inspiring, exhilarating, joyful, happy, in love with life, and what it has to offer, this is pure connection to your well-being, your worthiness.

Or your thoughts may be subdued apprehensive, fear based, or negative connotations; this is not connection to your well-being, but an indicator that your thoughts are pointing you in the wrong direction.

To increase the momentum of uplifting thoughts is to inspire the feeling within; welcome to Amplifying Thoughts and discover feelings and emotions.

Amplify and build up momentum to inspiring thoughts, this is the way to communicate with your greater part of you, your Inner Being, which is the Source of you.

'Conversations with Consciousness'

978-0-6483675-6-7 paperback

978-0-6483675-7-4 eBook

Vibrational frequency energy is the transference of energy from one object to another or converted into form, very much disbelieved unless they can see it or touch.

If conceivable and all the humans which populate this earth, were to realise they are all transmitting mechanisms, and have this powerful signal which is never detached from them and is holding every desire you wish to become a reality, wouldn't you really like to tap into this resourceful guidance system.

Wouldn't it be nicer to live in your desires – drive your desires – work in your desires – play in your desires – have the best relationships;

Welcome! You have just made the best decision to broaden your perspective and the continuing motion forward in the stimulation of thought.

'Back to Basics'

978-0-6483420-6-9 eBook

978-0-6483420-3-8 hardcover

978-0-6483675-0-5 paperback

This book focuses on inspiring the reader to examine alternatives to expensive chemical- based products. Discover how our common weeds are power-packed full of nutritional and medicinal healing. Learn to match the herb with the dish: which herbs to use in cooking. Learn how to make medicinal tinctures, poultice and herbal infusions. Have fun making natural alternatives for health, beauty and body products. Learn how to make mascarpone, sour cream, and ricotta. Have fun with these home recipes; you'll discover a new way to wellbeing.

'Back to Basics Harvest'

978-0-6483420-9-0 eBook

978-0-6483420-8-3 hardcover

978-0-6483675-1-2 paperback

161 recipes for creating chutneys, jams, vinaigrettes, sauces and jellies, just the way your grandmother used to, in the days when all good food was created in the home kitchen.

Suzanne Massee is passionate about home-grown and home-produced foods; her home-produced preserves have been sold throughout New Zealand.

Suzanne's restaurant was winner of the 2003 Wine and Food Challenge Award for Nelson-Marlborough – West Coast Region.

'Easy to Follow Baking Recipes'

978-0-6483675-2-9 eBook

This book is the outcome of years spent accumulating recipes, in a format that makes it easier to make the most of each season's harvests.

With easy to follow step by step recipes you can create delightful;

Baked Slices - Cakes - Biscuits - Christmas Cakes - Desserts - and Gluten Free recipes.

Added extra; how to make Dairy Products, did you know Mascarpone is so simple to make and yet so expensive to buy.

I had a cafeteria where I created the most delicious slices, the compliment of these slice recipes was through my father in-law who was the general manager and baker for a very popular bakery in Timaru in the South Island of New Zealand. These slice recipes have been handed down, and I have reduced the ingredient measurements from very large baker's trays to the household trays.

Social media

https://www.suzannemassee.com

https://www.amazon.com/-/e/B00DFBFRJK

https://www.smashwords.com/profile/view/suzannemassee

https://suzannemassee782038939.wordpress.com/blog/

https://www.facebook.com/massee19/

https://www.facebook.com/suzannem19/

https://www.instagram.com/suzanne.massee/

My positive momentum phrases

www.ingramcontent.com/pod-product-compliance
Lightning Source LLC
Chambersburg PA
CBHW071901290426
44110CB00013B/1234